Your

Father's

Voice

ALSO BY DAN ZEGART

Civil Warriors: The Legal Siege on the Tobacco Industry

Your Father's Voice

Letters for Emmy About Life with Jeremy—and Without Him After 9/11

LYZ GLICK *and*

DAN ZEGART

St. Martin's Press ⚏ New York

www.stmartins.com

ISBN 0-312-31921-5
EAN 978-0312-31921-2

First Edition: September 2004

10 9 8 7 6 5 4 3 2 1

For Jeremy and Emmy

Contents

Redemption of Sky

Soaring through the clouds
Arms spread, wind whisking on the back.
Unaffected by the laws of gravity,
One symbol of soul and freedom.
Disrupting the peace with a
Crack like thunder,
Lead whistled through the air.
Piercing pain,
Arms fold in,
The graceful glide metamorphoses
Into a chaotic dive.
The life meets the ground
And movement is no more.
But once again, Free.

—Jeremy Glick

First Light

Napping with Daddy. Emerson, one month old.

Dear Emmy,

I remember the morning after your father died.

When I awoke, I was upstairs at Grandma and Grandpa's house in the Catskills, a big, old, white clapboard farmhouse. I was in the brass bed and you were in your crib, right next to me. The first thing I saw when I opened my eyes was a pile of your daddy's clean clothes in a wicker basket. On the night table were a couple of his favorite CDs. I just started wailing. I could hardly get my breath I was crying so hard.

I sat up, put on my robe, trembling. The bedroom door was closed. I hoped I hadn't woken up the whole house. It was very early. Light was pouring in, the golden light of the sweetest part of the morning.

A close friend who lost her mom and dad in childhood had called the day before with advice: Get up quick, she said. Don't lie around in bed . . . thinking . . . remembering . . . *crying* . . .

It was good advice and I've followed it ever since, but I never counted on seeing so much of your dad's stuff lying around. So I managed to swing my feet onto the floor and wobble over to the railing of your crib, but I just kept crying harder and harder, because the daddy who loved you so fiercely, as fiercely as any man ever loved his tiny baby girl, was gone forever.

As I looked at you there, tucked under your little blue blanket, a mobile of white lambs turning slowly above your head, I was sick with anxiety, thinking you would know only a sad mother. I didn't want to imagine what it would be like for you to grow up without ever knowing your father. I felt like you'd truly lost both your parents the day before.

You were still tiny, just three months old. Born prematurely, you were small even for that age. So small! Who would protect you? Who would make you grin like your daddy did?

You lay on your back, eyes closed. Just then, from the bottom of a dream, you let out a delicate sigh, as though finishing a thought. Your cheeks crinkled up and you smiled ever so slightly at me. I cannot explain it, but at that moment I felt the power of something higher pulling me into something bigger than my pain. Your little shadow of a smile just took me over—like the sunlight from that window had gotten inside and warmed me. Like your father's energy was burning through the window. Your smile made me feel good enough to believe that maybe life could be good again. And then I remembered that the last time your father spoke to me, he said that for him to be at peace he needed us to be joyful.

By the time you're old enough to read this, everyone

will know the story of the men and women who tried to take back United Flight 93 from a gang of assassins who had already murdered people on the airplane and were bent on using it to kill a lot more people on the ground. What your father did in his last minutes of life made him a legend. You've heard that legend. Now I'm going to tell you your daddy's *story*. I mean the whole story of your very own father. Not just the ending, the part where the rest of the world found out about him. Because the truth is, the ending wasn't the best part or the worst part, it was just an ending.

I know your daddy wanted you to have his story. Pieces of it were scattered all over the place, as though it were inevitable that someday I'd go out and find them. Some were scribbled on legal pads in his room at home, or were tossed into the bottom drawer of the desk he had when he was a little boy, or were imprinted on film at Grandma and Grandpa's house. Some were little secrets his friends knew about him and never would have told me if he hadn't died. The world is seeded with traces of him. And in the year since he left us, I've been piecing it together, sometimes just by sitting here on our front porch thinking, like I'm doing now, looking out over Greenwood Lake while you sleep in your crib. And sometimes way off in places I didn't know even existed.

Since you're still too little to understand all this, I've put these letters into a book, like a birthday present you can't open for a long time. This is the master key, a gift of meaning. Here is your daddy's story.

—————

As the days rolled by after September 11th, I told myself that I'd done the hardest thing already: I'd said good-bye to your father, my soulmate, the only man I've ever loved.

I'll tell you more about our last telephone conversation later because its meaning will change once you know the whole story. But I can tell you that when your father called from Flight 93 and told me it had been commandeered by some "bad men," we knew exactly how to speak to each other, and we kept our heads—except for when he said, "I don't think I'm going to get out of this." He started sobbing so quietly that only I, who knew him so well, would have known he was crying. It made me feel terribly helpless because, except for the night you were born, I'd never heard your father cry.

Emmy, what I need you to understand is that your daddy and I managed to say enough to each other in twenty minutes on the telephone to bring our life together to an orderly conclusion. It didn't matter that in the few moments I had been awake I'd learned that airplanes were being rammed into the very center of government in Washington and the tallest skyscrapers in New York in an attack orchestrated by bloody-minded fanatics; or that four of those men were on Flight 93 and we both suspected, though we would never admit it to each other, that your daddy was probably right and would not survive.

Later, reporters asked me how we were able to help each other so effectively when we should have been paralyzed by fear. I told them I didn't know, and I didn't. Maybe now

I have a better idea. I know that the most important thing about that last telephone call wasn't the information I gave your father about what had happened in New York and Washington, although your daddy needed to know those things before he could decide whether to try to break into the cockpit and kill the hijackers; it wasn't even the few minutes we were able to spend talking about you and the future we would never have together. It was a few words said over and over, like a chant we repeated until it hung like a frozen rope between us. We said, "I love you." We said it so many times, I hear him saying it still.

I think your daddy always suspected he had a higher purpose. I don't believe it was any accident that Jeremy Glick was on Flight 93, although an accident—a fire at Newark airport—put him there, rather than on the flight he was to have taken the day before. It wasn't mere luck that an airline passenger with precisely the right physical skills to abort one of the 9/11 terror missions happened to be on the only plane hijacked that day where there was an opportunity to do so. There were four, five, six, maybe a dozen other passengers who fought the terrorists on Flight 93, and they all had plenty of nerve. Only your father had been taught the art of hand-to-hand combat from boyhood. To put it crudely, he had been trained to kill.

Emmy, your daddy was thirty-one when he died, had been married to me for just five years and knew you barely three months, yet I consider us blessed. He and I left nothing unsaid or undone and your father managed to give us everything we'll need to live out the rest of our days.

Of course, you've got to have a little luck. That's what Glick means in Yiddish—luck. I should point out, however, that the original Yiddish doesn't specify what kind. But if you meet the love of your life in high school, like I did, you've started off on the right foot.

Strong and Sweet

Judo champion! Jeremy—undated photo.

Dear Emmy,

I remember your daddy's hair.

It was what I noticed when I first laid eyes on him in ninth grade, on the first day of school, in early September 1984. We were in the same biology class, and I sat down next to him at a long lab table. He had an enormous Afro. It was too big for his head, like a bowl sitting above his ears, a real bush of curly dark-brown hair. And I thought to myself, *What is up with this kid's hair?*

I was feeling terribly insecure. First day of school, you don't know anyone. I had tried to sit with my brother, Pieter, at morning assembly but he didn't think it was cool to sit with his baby sister, so he ditched me.

And now I was sitting next to this kid who looked like an escaped cannibal.

But he was very sweet, made me feel comfortable right away. He said his name was Jeremy Glick—Jer to his friends.

I kidded him about his hair.

"My strength is in my hair," he said. "Just think of me as Samson with an Afro."

"I'm going to cut it off. Then I can do anything I want with you," I said.

We both laughed. He had a quick, crooked smile.

Our friendship was immediate and intense. He was funny. He had an agile mind. He was cool on his own terms. He wasn't a loudmouth or a druggie, and driving a Porsche and wearing the right shoes weren't any more important to him than they were to me. The teachers respected him, and as I got to know him, I began to realize that other kids looked up to him, even older kids. He didn't come on like a tough guy, but he was already the biggest kid at Saddle River Day School, a narrowly built six-footer who wore an earring shaped like a hatchet. We'd eat lunch together and snag odd moments during the school day to be with each other.

If he was a giant, I was a nymph: four-foot-ten and eighty pounds. I loved the fact that when I talked to him, he paid attention with his heart. And that he was protective— you never felt safer than when you were with Jeremy. I think he loved how different I was from him, that I was a lithe little thing who seemed made to be protected. And that I was warm. He craved warmth. We thought the same things were funny. Pomposity. People who were utterly unaware of how ridiculous they were—like men with huge potbellies wearing tiny shorts.

He went out for soccer and lacrosse and wrestling, at which he excelled, not surprisingly, since he had been one of New Jersey's top judo students from the age of six. He was a little shy and mumbled so badly that sometimes you barely caught what he said. Jimmy Best, who also was in our biology class and became friends with both of us, mumbled just as badly, and they had whole conversations I couldn't understand.

Jer was a mumbling fifteen-year-old gladiator with dark hair and eyes and slightly olive skin who eventually stopped mumbling and began to come out of his shell. I wasn't the only girl interested in him: Strong and sweet is a rare combination. I remember visiting my best girlfriend Diana Dobin and her toddler-age sister and their mother. I showed up in their kitchen with this extremely large-framed young man with a hatchet earring and a Mohawk (the Afro wasn't radical enough)—*somewhat* menacing in appearance. The little girl was listening to Raffi on the tape deck, and Jeremy started singing and doing a kind of cha-cha to Raffi, and it was funny, this dangerous-looking character boogying to "Baby Beluga."

When we couldn't do things together, we talked for hours on the phone. Every night, when he got back from judo and I returned from gymnastics, we'd call each other.

"I love you. You're my best friend," we'd say as we hung up.

I already had a boyfriend, but Jer hung around him so much that he became better friends with him than I was. And it was just so he could tag along with the two of us. Jer asked me out several times and by the time I said yes it had become inevitable.

As I remember it, we never seemed to get sick of being with each other. I had a little Volkswagen bug and we'd go to a diner for a greasy sandwich or lie around my room. I thought I'd found the perfect steady boyfriend.

Right from the start it was more than that to Jeremy.
"I've met the perfect girl," he told his mother.

In the beginning, it was a trio: Jennifer, Jonah, and Jeremy,
the three oldest Glick children. They played fantasy games together, superheroes in the woods in their backyard in Oradell,
breathlessly narrating their adventures. Jonah was the master
story-creator. Jennifer was the oldest, the ringmaster of the
circus. Jeremy acted everything out.

"And here comes the Hulk, jumping *out of the tree* onto
Aquaman . . ."

And Jeremy actually did come right *out of the tree* onto
Jonah.

The patch of woods behind the house seemed enormous
to them, the little driveway desperately steep when they
raced down it on their bikes, heading straight for the garage
door, sometimes failing to peel away in time and smacking
into the siding, leaving dents. Jeremy raced faster than any of
them and came closer to disaster, veering so sharply that the
elbow on his low side scraped pavement as he leaned into a
suicidally sudden turn. The house was a chocolate brown
colonial that looked small from the front. Jonah and Jeremy
had bunk beds and Jennifer had her own room next door.
The three of them whispered back and forth through the
vents, unheard by their parents, Lloyd and Joan, whose bedroom was above Jeremy and Jonah's room. (You know Lloyd
and Joan as Opa and Oma, which is Grandpa and Grandma
in Yiddish.) Windows were always broken both from play-
related accidents and because the two German shepherds,

Major and Minor, would rush the front window when they saw the mailman, which briefly led to a discontinuation of mail service due to a badly frightened mailman.

Jonah was the sensitive and brilliant mind, the problem-solver—as a child he never stopped talking. Jeremy could grab you with a story—but words were not fundamental to him. Jeremy did things. He was the kind of kid who would run into the middle of a living room full of adults with a huge smile on his face and hop around and sing. He loved music, and became proficient at the violin while in elementary school. There are pictures of him with the instrument tucked under his chin, pounding out the notes with a blissful grin and a bobbing Afro.

All the children had the first two initials JL, after Joan and Lloyd. Jennifer Lynn, Jonah Lyle, and Jeremy Logan— they were the top three. Then came the second two, Jared Lawrence and Jed Lowell, five years apart. And finally Joanna Leigh, born much later, when Jeremy's mother was already in her forties. When they went out to eat as a family, the waitress would ask Lloyd if they were all his, and he just puffed up; he loved hearing that. The Glick clan was numerous enough to be a self-sustaining, self-protective world. Although in fact, it wasn't just the Glicks, because the Glick kids often went places with the equally numerous Bangashes in the Glick station wagon, and when they stopped, children came running out like clowns from the clown car. Kim Bangash was the boy closest in age to Jeremy, and they became confidants. Everybody would wind up at Friendly's where Jer would order the giant Fribble, the one they served in a container the size of a bucket. This was a kid who would annihilate two full portions of dinner in a couple of minutes to get out the door to see his friends. Or wake up in the middle of the night just long enough to drain a quart of milk while standing in front of the refrigerator.

Opa and Oma stressed respect, a necessary virtue because otherwise things could get out of hand in a house with four strong boys. If you had to fight, you went to the mat in the den—Opa installed it for this very reason—and knocked each other around like little robots. A former army drill sergeant, Opa also nailed a chin-up bar to a doorframe and encouraged all the kids to do a couple of chin-ups every time they passed it. The boys grew fast, and Jeremy grew fastest. The top three got more and more competitive, and it spread to judo, wrestling, skiing, running, soccer, and swimming. "Let's race," someone would say. Competition was like breathing. It was, "let's see how far we can push this." Telling stories. Running to the store. Eating cereal. Faster, higher, wilder, flashier.

The three oldest boys never really got into sports like baseball and football and basketball because there wasn't enough physical contact. Instead, starting as young children, they went to Kokushi Dojo, a little warren of rooms above a car dealership in Westwood run by Sensei Nagayasu Ogasawara, a nationally respected Japanese judo master. Judo is the most exhausting of the martial arts and, next to jiu-jitsu, from which it is descended, the riskiest. It primarily emphasizes upright grappling via flips, throws, and holds, and the sparring is intensely physical. A judoka, or judo fighter, who is thrown and lands incorrectly can be seriously injured and broken limbs are not unheard of in adult competition. In addition to the sport, the boys soaked up the philosophy of judo, which is that the judoka's strength allows him to be gentle by choice, rather than from weakness. Sensei taught another lesson, as well: Be in control. Pin your opponent, don't depend on fickle judges for a decision on points. Master your behavior, on or off the mat.

All the Glick boys took to judo. For little Jeremy, it was demanding, exhausting, a little dangerous—everything he craved. It gave him discipline. It toughened Jonah. Jared fell in and became proficient, and Jed also studied with Sensei for a while. Kokushi Dojo was inexpensive and with both parents working, the boys were often there for hours every day. Judo became the Glick way of life. In the summer, the boys went to judo camp. The whole family would pile into Sensei's Maxivan and drive to Buffalo or Decatur for a tournament with Sensei and his daughter Liliko, later an international champion. These were the family vacations. Opa would drive anywhere in the United States for a match, completely dedicated to his boys' judo enthusiasm. Sensei was traditional and strict, the training unforgiving. He shouted, he ridiculed, he smacked the boys with kendo sticks—wooden swords—when they made mistakes. He could see they were tough. Jeremy was the toughest, and as they competed, quickly proved himself the best, winning his first championship at ten. His hallmark was aggression. He took control, and used everything he had—even his crown of hair.

"Before the match, when me and the other kid face off, I put my head down like this and shake my hair at him and it psychs him out," Jeremy told his mother.

Jeremy's role in the family was unique. Jared looked up to him. Jed worshiped him. He was the protector, even of

Jonah and Jennifer. And his parents knew this about Jeremy, knew they could rely on him absolutely. They entrusted Jeremy with monitoring his diabetic little brother Jared's diet at camp, and injecting him with insulin. He practiced on oranges for weeks to get the hang of it. The protector role spilled over into school as well. No one in their right mind would mess with the big kid carrying the "Desert Judo Champion" bookbag.

Of course, there's an exception to even the most sensible rule.

A classmate named Fred wouldn't stop fooling around at another classmate's bat mitzvah, even after Jeremy turned in his seat and gave him the weird one-eye-closed stare that meant you were in trouble. The next day, Jeremy cornered Fred in the student lounge before homeroom and with a kind of clinical detachment, pinned him to the floor. He said, quite deadpan, that he didn't want Fred doing that at his bar mitzvah, and then he let him up. It was done so dexterously, it awed Fred into respecting him.

Pieces, Parts, and Postcards

Emerson's First Christmas. Sitting with Grandpa,
December 2001.

Dear Emmy,

By the day after your father died, it was already obvious that the story of Flight 93 and Jeremy's part in it were well on their way to becoming a sensation, even among the spectacular events of September 11th. The phone rang constantly at my folks' place in the Catskills, and usually there was a reporter at the other end. I didn't want to talk to strangers. I wanted to think about your daddy, and I needed to be around people who also needed to think about him.

Two days after the crash, United Airlines sent two contact people up to Grandpa's house in Windham, New York. Their job was to provide help or information to our family and they were very kind, but there was no help they could give me, and information wasn't high on my immediate list of priorities. I was hell-bent on remaining ignorant not only about the precise details of what happened to Flight 93, but about any developments relating to September 11th. However, try as I might to steer clear of newspapers and the TV news, I was sitting in my bedroom at Windham with two girlfriends watching some innocuous program when footage of the Twin Towers collapsing flashed on the screen, as happened constantly that week. I would gladly have avoided seeing it. I already had a tape loop of my last conversation with your daddy spinning two dozen times a day in my head.

So when the airline people invited me to see the crash site in western Pennsylvania, my first impulse was to say no. But then I thought I might regret not going. Eventually, it would almost certainly matter. There was no denying that this thing had happened—and that this was where it happened. Perhaps I needed to go as a witness, so you could know about it.

Since I wouldn't fly, United sent three black limousines to collect us and the Glicks. My limo also contained Grandpa and Jim Best and Kim Bangash, friends of mine and Jeremy's since high school. I called them my posse because they protected me from threats to my equilibrium. My posse was with me almost constantly in the days immediately following the disaster—being interviewed en masse for *Dateline,* at Jeremy's memorial service the Sunday after the crash, and now this. We drove all day except to stop and breast-feed you, at which point I ordered a compliant posse out of the car. Almost eight hours later, we arrived at a ski resort near Shanksville, Pennsylvania, a rural hamlet near Pittsburgh, where they were putting up all the Flight 93 victims' families. Staying at a ski resort was like a bad joke because Jeremy and I loved skiing together more than just about anything. *Great,* I thought. *Another thing I'll never want to do again.* I picked at my dinner and went to bed.

The next morning, September 20th, the dining room

was filled with Flight 93 families and officials, including the coroner. I had handed off dealing with the details of the investigation of the crash to Grandpa and Kim Bangash and Grandma's brother Joe, who didn't come to Shanksville but had provided the coroner with Jeremy's underwear and razor for DNA matching, while our dentist sent dental records in case they found his teeth.

I was eating breakfast when the coroner walked up to Grandpa. I didn't learn about the conversation until later:

"We've identified your son-in-law," he said. "We have a small amount of remains. Teeth, actually."

He said Jeremy had been among the first twelve people identified.

Grandpa clapped his hand on the coroner's shoulder.

"Thank you for that," he said. "But I'd appreciate it if you'd stay away from my daughter."

Tour buses appeared to ferry us to the crash site. Jer and I always avoided bus tours on vacations. I wanted to be alone with my memories, not herded in with a mass of others. Although I felt for them as comrades in a common hurt, to me they were, nevertheless, strangers. And I simply had nothing to say to them.

I asked if the bus had seat belts. It didn't.

"My daughter's in a car seat and it needs a seat belt to attach to. You'll need to get me my own bus."

Which they did—the only passengers were you, me, Kim, Jim, and Grandpa.

It was raining. Our short caravan of buses passed miles of people who stood in the rain and watched us go by, waving little flags and crying. There were two security gates on the road leading to the crash site. At the first gate were reporters and TV cameras with big microphones covered with fake-fur windscreens. The second gate marked the entrance to a dirt and gravel road that had been built so a battalion of experts and equipment operators could get to the field where the plane struck the earth.

The buses stopped. The land around us was part of a reclaimed strip mine and scattered about were the rusting hulks of mine machinery. We got out and walked down the dirt road until we came to a low bluff. A canopy shielded us from the rain and wind. Under the canopy was a makeshift memorial on hay bales—letters, photographs, poems, books, flowers, little figurines, stuffed animals, baby shoes.

A field of tall yellowing grass framed by woods lay below us, with a farm behind it. The trees at the back of the field were burnt black and stripped of leaves and branches. Bright orange plastic flags marked where a bit of painted steel, a melted driver's license, a seat-belt buckle, a tooth, a shoe, a gold ring, or a bit of bone had been found. Aside from a thousand-pound piece of a jet engine, which landed in a nearby pond, the earth so far hadn't yielded anything bigger than a few inches in length, I learned later. The plane had come down at a forty-five-degree angle, hitting the ground at roughly the speed of sound, which snapped the cockpit off from the fuselage and sprayed the woods with fire. Most of the aircraft and its contents were pulverized into small, coarse, hot pieces that disappeared into a smoldering, blackened crater. There was no wreckage. There was nothing to see.

We weren't allowed to walk down to the field because it was still considered a crime scene. The hole in the ground wasn't visible, but you could see trucks and bulldozers around it. Human remains were found in both the field and the scorched woods. In this case, remains meant anything containing human DNA.

There was little conversation on the bluff among the few dozen of us from the victims' party, which was engulfed by hundreds of Red Cross volunteers in red vests dispensing soda and candy and little Red Cross tissue packets. We put the things we had brought for your father down on the hay bales: a "Got Milk?" poster, because he drank so much milk; sunflowers, our wedding flower; pictures of you with Daddy and me with Daddy; a Beanie Baby pug, for our two pugs. I left him a letter. It was written in a moment of blind grief and I can't remember a word of it.

We were at the crash site for an hour and a half—far too long. As soon as I got there, I realized this place had nothing to do with Jeremy. He had merely passed through and now it didn't matter. It was just a cold, rainy field in the Allegheny mountains. It didn't need people. Like me, it wanted to be left alone.

When my arms got tired of holding you, we passed you back and forth among us and waited for the buses. Finally we left. On the bus I was thinking that I was glad there was no body, that there was truly nothing left. If there had been, I would have felt like saying to Jeremy, *Why didn't you keep breathing? You should have kept breathing.*

I had gone to the field frightened at what I might see, and I was comforted by the feeling that your father wasn't in such a remote, gray place. I knew he was telling me not to waste my time standing in the rain looking for him.

———

Instead of going back to the hotel, we were shuttled off to an old country lodge where we sat in rows in a big wooden room near the entryway. A minister and Lynne Cheney, wife of Vice President Dick Cheney, gave unmemorable speeches. *Why am I here? We already had a memorial service,* I thought. The room had a high ceiling and a big window. I gazed out the window and watched the wind blow through the trees and cried some more. You drank your milk.

Next door was a dining room and, after an hour, we all milled in there. There was some confusion about whether everyone in our party would be able to sit together—I had my posse, the Glicks had Jeremy's brothers and sisters, plus their children, spouses, and girlfriends. A complex discussion ensued.

"Here's where I'm sitting," I announced from a chair. I had no energy for arranging the furniture.

We broke into two parties at adjacent tables and ate pasta. Afterward, Lynne Cheney came by with her daughter and offered condolences. I felt she was completely sincere, but your father would have said—correctly—that this was still politics. Thousands of people came out into the rain to cry with us. That couldn't be denied, it was real. And maybe Jeremy provided, if not a triumphal moment, at least an even draw against tall odds, which made a lot of people feel better somehow.

A woman came up to me. Did Jeremy mention her brother? He was a big guy and Jeremy said there were three other big guys planning to attack the cockpit with him. She described him. I didn't have much to offer her, because Jeremy said very little about other passengers. We had been too interested in each other.

"You know what, your brother was probably there," I told her. "Sounds like that would make sense."

I was grateful for how much I knew about how your father spent his last moments. So many people vanished without a trace that morning and no one will ever know how or where or why. I knew where and roughly how, and it was beginning to dawn on me that I wanted to know—that I *needed* to know—why.

Since our party had its own little bus, we were able to hurry back to the resort right after dinner to settle in and put a period on this long, strange, official day. Once back at the hotel, I decided on a massage, one of my favorite luxuries. *This will be relaxing.* Within minutes of lying down under the towel, I was limp, out of control and sobbing. I tried to hide it, but thought, *the masseur probably knows we're all a bunch of widows and orphans staying at the hotel.* It just wasn't in me to confide in a stranger, though.

I was glad it was a short massage or I'd have been bawling like a calf. Afterward I made what I intended to be a beeline for Jim and Kim's room. I wanted a beer and fellowship, and I wanted them badly. I had Grandpa watching you, so the coast was clear. The Seven Springs Resort is enormous, full of oddly arranged corridors and nooks and it seemed that around every corner was a Flight 93 person, including multiple Glicks and strangers with something to

say. It was part of what had been going on all day. Everyone
wanted to be around me and talk to me, either because they
were in pain or because I was some kind of touchstone for
the whole experience of September 11th. But I had nothing to give them. Not a tear, not a smile, not a single volt of
emotion. I was just trying to hold it together out in the
hallway because I felt like I hadn't been able to grieve or
think about your daddy or talk freely or think clearly all
day. I'd been a public widow for twenty-four hours and I
was heartily sick of it.

"Oh Jimmy, I need a beer," I said when I burst in through
his door and dumped myself on the couch.

"God, you do," said Jimmy, and popped up to get me
one.

The next day, the limousines drove us to our house in Hewitt, New Jersey. I felt I couldn't do many more events like
the crash site memorial, I was too raw. I had already turned
down an invitation from the White House to attend a special
joint session of Congress at which President Bush would
talk to the country about September 11th. They offered to
fly us there in a military jet. I told them no, and that Lisa
Beamer, whose husband Todd also fought the Flight 93 hijackers, would do nicely as a representative for all of us,
which she did. I knew this wouldn't be my last invitation to
Washington, and it was time for you and me to go home.

Jimmy Best and my friends Ana and Shari stayed with
me for a couple of days and slept in the living room like

we were back in college. This was the first time I'd been at the house on Greenwood Lake since your daddy left for the airport, so I found a kind of time capsule of his last hours in the house. A paper coffee cup with a piece of chewed gum in it, the pizza box from his dinner, a reminder note to pack white T-shirts. For some reason, seeing his clothes in the dryer knocked the wind out of me. I stared at the dryer for an hour, unable to decide what to do with his laundry.

Some things were oddly reassuring. Never completely finishing a glass of milk was a little trademark of Jer's and there were several glasses around with a finger or so still on the bottom. I drove to the one-room office he had rented just before you were born, a mile away above a restaurant, and cleaned it out. Jeremy's filing technique consisted of heaping piles of paper on folding tables. In his desk I discovered a drawer filled with lip balms, every flavor and variety. On top was a series of books—a guide for new fathers on how to raise a child. The volume on infants was missing. He must have taken that to read on the plane.

My incursion into your father's private spaces stopped with his dresser. I decided to give each of his brothers and close friends one of his ties. I was going to give his clothes to the Goodwill. Instead I bagged them and stored them on the sun porch so you'd have one more clue about your daddy. I never did look in his closet. For some reason, the idea of going in there still gives me a chill.

———

As soon as I got home, I had to deal with the logistics of a husband who'd died in a plane crash, and become famous for it. There were all sorts of consequences. I had to visit a lawyer to go over our will. Our car had to be returned from the airport where the FBI had impounded it, and the local police were kind enough to pick it up in Newark and deliver it to our door. The phone was clogged with well-wishers, reporters, and friends. As to the reporters, at least you knew what the rules were. If you said no, they were supposed to leave you alone, and if they didn't, you kept saying no until they did. The vast majority of strangers meant and acted well. Most communicated—quite respectfully—by mail. Thousands of letters, cards, and gifts began arriving from the well-wishers. The sun porch at the front of the house became the "9/11 Room," filling up with the most random assortment of objects—T-shirts with and without sayings, quilts, toys, a carved eagle that appeared on the front steps along with a poem by Emerson on a laminated sheet of paper, artwork, appliances, and dozens of Bibles, some sprouting scraps of paper marking recommended passages.

Two Vietnam veterans sent their Purple Hearts, an extraordinary, touching gesture. Yet I wanted to say to them, this is not what Jeremy and I were about. Jeremy didn't sign up to fight terrorism. His was an act of love, not war. He did what he did because he wanted so very badly to come home to his wife and baby daughter. A couple of the gifts really upset me. Someone sent a bumper sticker that said, " 'Let's roll': Todd Beamer's last words to Jeremy Glick." The last words of a young man blown out of the world in the prime of life don't belong on a bumper sticker. Or there was the local man who took to sending us a Beanie Baby at each holiday with a card saying, "Love, Daddy." Eventually, I started hurling them across the room. *Couldn't you just sign them, "From a friend"?*

Aside from those things, I saved almost everything people sent, thinking it would create a tangible connection to September 11th for you, perhaps a more objective one than I could offer with my memories and stories. I started pasting the letters into three books that you could read someday— one for friends' letters and two others for well-wishers. Those quoting Psalms and saying we're all sinners being punished by God went into a special envelope Grandpa and I called "the overly religious file."

Some of the well-wishing was quirky to say the least. Several people felt connected to me solely because their names happened to be Jeremy Glick. A bunch of them telephoned, including a paralyzed Australian who rang while I was feeding you dinner. He went on and on about how he wanted to send you a gift, and by the time he hung up you'd fallen asleep, your dinner unfinished.

As I began to sort through things in the house, anything containing Jeremy's voice or image seemed infinitely precious. It turned out there weren't nearly as many pictures of you with Daddy as I'd hoped. You don't take pictures thinking that's all you'll have left. However, his cell phone hadn't been turned off, and I found myself ringing up to hear his voice—calm and deep, very comforting—on the recorded message. I confessed this to Jimmy Best one night and he told me he'd been doing it, too. I phoned Kim to laugh about it with him, and Kim had also been calling. Plus Jeremy's mother and sister.

"Now what?" I asked Kim. "Do we all start leaving messages for each other?"

Kim, Jimmy, Diana, Shari, Ana—we'd been a close circle of friends before, and here we were embarked on something new, bound closer still by rules that made sense perhaps only to us.

I was doubly glad to find Jer on the cell phone because there were certain things I couldn't locate. I couldn't find any recent videotapes of Jeremy, much less of Jeremy and you. I wasn't even sure there were any. It bugged me. There were other keepsakes and talismans I was looking for, but that was the biggest, and in order that I wouldn't become some kind of grief-crazed obsessive-compulsive, I limited my searching to twenty minutes a day.

But that's what you do with death—you seek what's missing. You go down through the layers, through a geology of absence. The first layer is him, his presence. That living, breathing person who's with you—physically warping the air next to you at the dinner table, or lying on the couch watching TV with our pugs, Eloise and Maxine, snuggled in next to him, and all eighteen inches of you, Emmy, snoozing face-down on his chest. I'd walk by and he'd say, "Take pictures, take pictures. You've gotta get this." Because you'd have a little smile on your face, or you'd be in some strange splayed position, with one arm sticking out.

Then, too, I missed that other mind who matched my little one-liners with his own, with whom I shared a sense of fun. Now I'd be driving somewhere and think of something clever and say to myself, "Oh, Jer, you're missing it. That was a good one."

Of course, there are many more layers in the geology of absence. A big one was having someone else to help take care of this little baby who was keeping me up much of the night, so that in addition to having lost my husband and being hounded by well-wishers and reporters, I was a barely functioning, sleep-starved, neurotic wreck who cried twenty times a day because she was on the verge of physical collapse. Your daddy had been so devoted to both of us, he'd get up repeatedly to feed you in the middle of the night so I could sleep. Since you were born a month prematurely, not only did you wake up every hour and a half to feed, but you hadn't yet developed any sucking reflex. So Jeremy taped a little tube to his pinky, put it in your mouth, and used a small syringe to pump milk into you. He simply loved feeding you. "This way I get to bond with her right away," he'd say. I called him "Daddy Milk-Fingers."

One day that fall, I was in a fairly blank state of mind, wandering around the house trying to finish some chore, when I happened to look under the desk in my office on the second floor, and there was the battery charger for our ancient video camera, plugged into the wall, happily charging away. I was jubilant because I'd been looking for weeks for this piece of hardware, without which I couldn't use the camcorder. I immediately replaced the batteries, hit eject, and a tape popped out of the camera. I ran downstairs and put it in the VCR. And sure enough it was Daddy and you.

I'd never seen it before. Jeremy must have shot it himself

some afternoon when he was alone with you. You're lying on the changing table. It opens with a close-up of your head, mouth open, wailing, but you quiet as soon as he starts talking:

"Hello pretty baby—oh, no, no, don't cry." He strokes your cheek and the top of your head.

"This is just the camera. Hello. Today Emmy's six weeks old. It's her birthday today. Hello. Helloooo! Hellooo!"

He keeps caressing you—your head, your arms. Your dark eyes stare at him.

"Say hello, Emmy. Say hello to everyone. Say hello. Teenie little body. Little feet. Little feet. Little toes. Oh, she says hello! Hello! Hello! Hello! What are you thinkin'? We just went for a walk. A nice walk. Then we changed your diaper. Then we're going to give you some food, because I know you're hungry, but we're hanging out right now . . . Little cutie. . . . She's got lots of hair now."

He keeps stroking the top of your head.

"I know you think that milk comes from fingers, but it doesn't," he laughs.

I'm aware that a videotape might be kind of cheating in the spirituality department, but I'd never felt more like giving thanks to God in all my life. It was like getting a postcard from heaven. *Everything's fine up here. I'm the same guy you remember. Arranged this little surprise for you. Love, Jeremy.* I cried—of course. And I was euphoric, overjoyed, stoned on this new, unexpected glimpse of you with Daddy. Something important had been given to me. I had already realized your daddy wasn't with the bits and pieces and parts in Shanksville. Now it came in a kind of warm flash that it wasn't going to be hard being home, it was going to be easy. Maybe not right away, but eventually. This was where the memories were. Here our past together still ran into the present, like an old movie that's over but is still flapping away on its reel on the projector, waiting for someone to turn it off.

And it dawned on me that if your father could turn up like this here in the house, he might be other places I'd never thought of looking for him.

The Little Man
Makes a Move

High school sweethearts, fall 1988.

Dear Emmy,

When I first met your father, one of the things we had in common was a love for the pure physical thrill of athletics. For me, it was gymnastics, and for Jeremy, it was judo, but I soon realized he was a lot more serious about his sport than I was about mine, even though I'd been a gymnast since I was five. Judo trophies filled his bedroom at home, which was just a few miles from Upper Saddle River, where I lived. Not long after we met, Jer took third place in the junior nationals, yet he never even mentioned it. Not to me, not to any of his friends. He didn't talk about judo at all. Humility is central to its philosophy, and he took his judo too seriously to brag about it.

I did see his matches with the wrestling team, where he was nicknamed the Hulk. Jonah also wrestled, but by high school Jeremy had outgrown Jonah, wrestling in the 160-pound-weight class while Jonah, three years older, was just over a hundred pounds. Jonah was a technically proficient wrestler, but Jer's killer instinct made him more exciting to watch. His hatred of losing was so deep, it allowed him to prevail over stronger, more experienced competitors, and so he rarely lost. Jer was famous for his "standing take-downs:" pulling a wrestler off his feet so quickly that the contest was over before it began. He was at his best in a close match where he had to really fight for his life. Then he'd fall back on his bread and butter—the acrobatic flips and other judo moves, although judo's potentially deadly choke holds and pressure points are taboo in wrestling.

He trained hard, but it was more than training. Jer had been bred for combat. In addition to the strong emphasis on physical culture in the Glick household, the competition with his brothers, and the judo camps, Jeremy and his best friend Kim Bangash spent three summers at the Iowa Intensive Wrestling Camp, grueling month-long programs run by Dan Gable, an Olympic gold medalist and one of the sport's legends.

Basketball games usually drew the largest audiences of the winter sports at Saddle River Day School. One day there was no game, and the entire school showed up to watch the wrestlers in the main auditorium. The opposition was Storm King, a large private school whose wrestling squad far outclassed that of little Saddle River Day School, whom the Storm King'ers saw as soft little preppies.

When Jer hit the mat, the energy of the room revved him up to a kind of fever pitch. His opponent was big, and far from soft, with muscles like Spider-Man. He and Jer leaned into each other. Jer was in trouble from the beginning, and the point totals became more and more lopsided against him. Then the other wrestler made a small mistake, just a little lapse of concentration as he committed to a move, and I saw Jeremy almost break into a smile, as though he had somehow sensed this would happen. There was a blur of hands. The next thing anybody knew, Jeremy had Spider-Man suspended over his head like a sheet of plywood. He held him there momentarily, then crashed him heavily into the floor, professional-wrestling style. The whole gym roared when they saw the guy go up in the air, and pandemonium erupted when he hit the mat. Jeremy lost the match—narrowly—on points, but Storm King never took Saddle River for granted again, and the following year, Jeremy won every match he entered and took fourth place in the nationals.

Jeremy did well in school, and in the subjects about which he was passionate, like English, he did remarkably well. He loved to write—stories, poems, letters. And he loved to read, Ralph Waldo Emerson being a particular favorite. Something about Emerson's thorny individualism rang true for Jer. He could recite Emerson by heart, especially the poem "On Success":

To laugh often and much;
To win the respect of intelligent people and the af-
    fection of children;
To earn the appreciation of honest critics and endure
    the betrayal of false friends;
To appreciate beauty, to find the best in others;
To leave the world a bit better, whether by a healthy
    child, a garden patch or a redeemed social condi-
    tion;

To know even one life has breathed easier because
   you have lived.
This is to have succeeded.

A locomotive couldn't drag Jer into working at something he didn't enjoy, yet he had no shortage of intellect and
so he was one of the top students at Saddle River Day. But
high school was not an easy time for your father. Friends
who had known him from childhood thought he became a
bit hardened as a teenager, a little sad. I didn't see that side of
him, yet I knew he was constantly in trouble with his parents, which took a toll. He had a mischievous, reckless
streak, a poor match for a serious-minded Jewish family of
four brothers and two sisters in which money was tight and
everyone was expected to buckle down and work hard and
not waste time.

It's always tougher for older siblings, but Jonah and Jennifer
didn't challenge their parents the way Jeremy did. He tended
to charge them head-on. Stubborn. Wouldn't back down. He
was a big, strong, intense, angry kid who had about a million
volts of energy going through him. Any family would just
about have to throw a lasso over him to make him behave,
and there probably wasn't one in the world, let alone New
Jersey, that could do it. And the Glicks certainly couldn't.

They tried, though. They were plenty strict. He would
want to go out at night to see me, and they'd refuse to
let him. So he'd sneak out anyway. Or he'd creep out of
the house after midnight to go off with Jimmy Best and
Kim Bangash on some crazy mission—they called them
all-nighters—pushing his dad's Cadillac up the Glicks'

driveway so they could start it without anyone hearing. Once, they stripped naked, switching seats at every light. They slept under a bridge in the middle of winter, shivering under newspapers. Your father was just looking for some fun in the middle of the night. But the end result was that he would be confined to his room. To fight off going stir-crazy, he'd practice juggling or spinning a yo-yo for hours on end until he was expert.

Since Jeremy was so often in trouble at home, we spent a lot of time at my house. My family was small, and goofing around was the norm, especially between me and my dad. I was a daddy's girl, and was almost never punished. Grandpa was good with young people. He'd find some gory headline from the *New York Post*—"Father Kills Teenager with Ax"— and tape it to the refrigerator to tease us. Jeremy and Grandpa liked each other right away.

Things between Jeremy and his own father were more complicated, but there was no question in anyone's mind that there was love at its center. Jeremy looked up to his father, wanted to learn from him. Even with all the conflict, they still talked, and they still took trips together, like a judo junket to Florida when Jer was seventeen. Despite a grueling training regimen, he lost to someone who really wasn't as good as he was.

They had flown to Florida, and on the way home Jer was furious about dropping the match. Opa just let Jeremy talk it out.

"I don't understand how it happened. I never even considered losing," Jer said. "It never crossed my mind."

"Maybe that's why he won," said Opa. "He knew he'd

probably lose, so he was more relaxed, and he just let himself go for it."

Jer thought about that while the countryside below rolled by under the wing of the plane.

"It really is better to consider all the possibilities," he said finally.

By his senior year, the cycle of rebellious acts that lead to escalating tension with his parents was infecting our relationship. He was the leader of the wolf pack and, by my more conservative standards, he was on the verge of spinning out of control. He started making trips into New York City with Jimmy Best or one of the other pals, going to clubs, staying out most of the night.

The thing was, Emmy, even your father's worst teenage episodes had a strange way of showing how unselfish he was. For instance, there was The Party—the only one Jeremy had at his house during high school—at which Kim Bangash jumped into the Glick family Cadillac—*Lloyd's* Cadillac— and did donuts on the street in front of the house until black smoke belched not only from the tailpipe but from pretty much everything behind the rear window. A dull clunk was heard as the transmission exploded, dumping bits of metal and reddish fluid onto the ground, and the car swayed gently to a halt. The Party was over. Your father accepted the blame for the Cadillac's final minutes, though he'd had nothing to do with it.

Jeremy's dad also had a beat-up maroon Datsun sedan. It wasn't long after the Cadillac disaster that Jeremy borrowed the Datsun, without parental permission, to drive himself and a classmate named Gillian, a beautiful and gifted dancer, into New York City to see a play as part of an English-class field trip. As they drove along the left lane of the narrow, twisty West Side Highway, they were sideswiped by another car. The little Datsun bounced off the divider and rolled over onto the passenger side of the car. The window on Gillian's side exploded, and unlike Jeremy, she wasn't wearing a seat belt. Bracing himself with one hand against the somersaulting car, Jeremy grabbed the back of her pants with the other and somehow managed to throw her into the backseat. The Datsun came to rest, upside down in the breakdown lane on the right side of the road.

When Gillian's mother showed up to see her at the hospital, Jeremy apologized over and over again for the accident, but it was eventually acknowledged by everyone that if he hadn't yanked her from the front seat, she would have been hurled out the window to her death.

Upon returning home, Jeremy was in trouble for taking—and destroying—yet another of his father's cars, and nearly killing someone else in the process. Yet, viewed another way, the net result, the part everyone would remember and marvel at for years to come, was that he had actually *saved* a human life. Something many of us will never do, he had done before his eighteenth birthday, and accomplished it with real style, a full-blown snatch from the grave worthy of a judoka. Even his most perilous misadventures had a way of kicking up a small glitter of gold. It was as though he had the power to stop the truly bad things from happening. A kind of magic, perhaps.

I had an easier time of it than Jeremy growing up. Opa was a computer programmer who got into the field in the late sixties, the vacuum tube days, and although he did very well at a series of sizable companies, he had a big family to support. Your grandpa founded a successful market research company, and since there were only two children, Pieter and myself, we could do things like go to Europe on vacations. The Makely household always emphasized education over possessions, though, just as Jeremy's family did.

With Jeremy and I on tenuous ground, I was planning to accompany Grandpa to England for winter break of senior year, and he and I drove into New York to get my passport. When we got back, I ratted on his bad habits to your grandma.

"Mom!" I said. "You should see how much coffee Dad drinks and how many cigarettes he smoked at work today."

"Oh, Richard. What do you think that's doing to your heart?" she scolded my father.

They drove up to the Windham house for the weekend. The next day, Saturday, I went to see Jeremy wrestle in Newark. I was coming down with the flu and I wouldn't let him stay over at my house that night. So I was alone when around dawn the next morning, I awoke to hear someone tiptoeing around downstairs. Soft footsteps started up the stairs. I opened my door slowly and peeked into the hall. It was Uncle Joe.

He apologized for letting himself in.

"Your dad's in the hospital. He had some kind of indigestion," he said. I burst into tears. It was such an obvious cover-up.

Uncle Joe got Jeremy on the phone, and he gave him the unvarnished version: The indigestion had been a symptom of a major heart attack that had put my dad in intensive care at Albany Medical Center. Now I was really out of control, which Jeremy could hear even from where he was. He said he'd be right over. His parents ordered him to stay home and do his homework. He was not to leave the house.

"I have to go to the hospital with Lyz. Her dad is really sick. I don't know when I'll be back," Jeremy said. And he walked out.

When we arrived at the hospital they had Dad on a stretcher, moving him from one room to another. His face was blue and he was covered with white tape and plastic tubes. It did not look good.

Jer and I went for a walk outside. He told me that his brother Jonah had gotten a rare blood infection a few years earlier and it was very serious, but it all changed quickly and soon he was home again.

"You know what? Sometimes things, even when they look so bad, they're going to turn out okay," he said.

I was a little pissed off at this: *Look, we have no clue at all what's going to happen, so if it's all the same to you, this is where I cry for an hour.* But he meant it, and he kept saying it like he actually knew which way things were going to go, because he'd been through it all before. The sheer weight of his certainty began to drive out my fear, though he was probably as upset and scared as I was.

Grandpa had an angioplasty and was in the hospital a long time, but recovered fully. He was only forty-seven. He slowed down after that, and retired—temporarily—from business. I had the house in Saddle River to myself because he and Grandma moved up to Windham while he recuperated. Jeremy was around a lot, and the heart attack certainly brought us closer, at least for a while. Mom and Dad came home periodically, leaving a check for groceries, with which we bought Cheez Whiz, Steak-Ums, Ding Dongs, and Ring Dings for gluttonous binges. All my friends and anyone we knew who needed a place to stay lived at my house that spring.

Not even a steady diet of junk food could hide the deterioration Jeremy and I felt in our relationship. By the time we'd been anointed prom queen and king, we were on the verge of breaking up. He was to attend the University of Rochester in upstate New York, and I was going to Colby College, in the deep woods of Maine. I wanted to explore and have my own life. And he had gotten a little too wild. I couldn't see that aspect being much improved by a long-distance romance.

Jeremy was not happy about breaking up. He brooded. We argued. The last straw took place at a party not long before graduation, when Jeremy kissed a friend of mine and I physically attacked her. Just because we were going to be away from each other didn't mean I was going to put up with some girl fooling around with him right in front of me.

So off went Jeremy to college, without the girlfriend with whom he'd been obsessed since the first day of high school. Within hours of his arrival at Rochester, things got worse when his parents rummaged through his belongings and found pot. There was suddenly a real rift between Jeremy and his folks, one that no one wanted to talk about even in later years. Contact was broken off. Jeremy felt, perhaps for the first time in his life, completely alone.

My first semester at college was spent in Dijon, France, where Colby College had an exchange program. So I had a somewhat limited awareness of all the circumstances with Jeremy, but I knew enough to offer him sympathy via care packages stuffed with cookies and cigarettes. Although things were difficult for him, somehow for the two of us it was more a bittersweet experience. He wrote me beautiful multipage letters and we had long, inebriated trans-Atlantic phone calls—him on beer, me on red wine.

Jer used to talk on the phone about how sometimes he felt we were chess pieces being moved around by the Little Man. The Little Man put a tremendous amount of energy into his schemes, he tried to get us lined up with each other, but he just wasn't the brightest guy and things kept going wrong. Somehow I wound up in France while Jeremy went to Rochester. But someday, someway, the Little Man would get us back together.

"He's really trying," Jer said. "Maybe there's other pieces he'll have to move around before it can happen."

"Maybe he's been drinking even more than we have," I said.

"Drunk Little Man," he said.

"Drunk *omnipotent* Little Man," I said.

"Scary," he said.

His letters to me were whimsical and filled with longing. He had published six poems in our high school literary magazine, but I never paid attention to them until he sent me copies with his letters. Two were love poems clearly inspired by me—one used his nickname for me, "Baby Blue," as its title. Others were coming from another place entirely, a location far away, a long, cold call from somewhere in the future:

Redemption of Sky

> Soaring through the clouds
> Arms spread, wind whisking on the back.
> Unaffected by the laws of gravity,
> One symbol of soul and freedom.
> Disrupting the peace with a
> Crack like thunder,
> Lead whistled through the air.
> Piercing pain,
> Arms fold in,
> The graceful glide metamorphoses
> Into a chaotic dive.
> The life meets the ground
> And movement is no more.
> But once again, Free.

> —Jeremy Glick

My House to the White House

The Glick family visits the White House,
December 2001.

Dear Emmy,

Being at the Greenwood Lake house had its comforts, but it was still lonely, and I had you to nourish and care for, which would have been plenty of responsibility even if I'd been sharing it with Jeremy. And I had to get you to *sleep*. It had been Jeremy who could always induce you—through some combination of soothing, stroking, customized sounds (water, electric fan, whale songs), and most of all, stretching you out on his chest like a kitten—to fall asleep. I called him Sandman. He was just really good at it. Don't ask me why.

Now I was Sandman. It was very much a case of, *be* Sandman or forget about getting any rest myself. Beginning the day after Jer died, I rocked you to sleep in the blue rocking chair he had bought. All my friends were saying, "You gotta let her cry it out. It will be best for you. Babies have to learn to fall asleep." But I couldn't put you down and let you cry yourself to sleep. I felt you'd already lost so much and I wanted to comfort you. I didn't want you to feel insecure. And Jer would never, ever let you cry in your bed.

We slept together from the day after Jer died. You slept *so* much better with me. Around this time, I remember our pediatrician asked me how you were getting through the night.

"Much better now that she's in my bed," I said.

"I'm not for cosleeping," he said.

"Is it okay with you if I do what I have to do to get a little more sleep?"

That won me a look. Sympathy.

"Whatever's best for the both of you," he said.

I was glad to have my pediatrician's support, because aside from my own ingenuity, the only thing I had in this great wide world to help get you to sleep was a metal frame chair covered with cloth that vibrated and played music when you hit a button. The bouncy chair really worked, and when all else failed, I'd put you in it, flip the switch, and give thanks to God that eighty-nine cents worth of plastic circuitry had somehow become imbued with the power to send you to dreamland. This chair had a history. Jer and I used to stick it in the middle of the dinner table, like a floral centerpiece, so you could be right there with us while we ate. When we barbecued with friends, you'd be in the bouncy chair up on the picnic table, or vibrating away close by if it was nap time. What an appliance. I kept it by the side of the bed in case you woke up.

Needless to say, I didn't go anywhere without the bouncy chair. So when I got an invitation to a memorial at the White House for all the Flight 93 families, just a few days after I got back from Shanksville, one of my major concerns was whether I could bring along the bouncy chair, whose metal frame didn't fold for transport. And for the several moments when it wasn't clear if it would fit in the car with the rest of the baby stuff, the White House trip was definitely in jeopardy. Because nowhere in the executive branch of government was there anything to replace the bouncy chair.

I was actually relieved to be leaving the Greenwood Lake house and going off on this White House trip, which I was making with the Glicks, and for which, unlike the Pennsylvania trip, the ceremonial portion promised to be mercifully brief. I didn't feel up to returning to work at the business college in New York City where I'd been teaching social sciences before the crash. Still, I had to keep doing *something*. Long spells of empty time were a slow-acting poison for me.

Not that I was particularly agog at the idea of going to the White House or seeing the president. I've never been impressed by celebrity, and I'd been there a couple of years earlier during the Clinton presidency while working in public relations. I still wasn't up to flying, so once again, a limousine was provided for you, me, and a somewhat shrunken posse consisting of Grandpa, my brother Pieter, and Jim Best. We stayed overnight at the Phoenix Park Hotel, my first night alone in a hotel room without Jeremy. The TV was on all night keeping me company. At breakfast the next morning, Jed Glick was eating at the next table, and I could see Jeremy in Jed so clearly in that moment that I broke down over my cornflakes.

We had to hurry to get to the White House on time. It was raining, so the ceremony was held inside the White House, instead of in the Rose Garden. Just after entering the building, we were ushered into a small library off to the right where the Flight 93 people were gathered. I didn't talk to anyone, but busied myself inspecting the portraits of presidents on the walls. I paused in front of Teddy Roosevelt, for whom I've always felt a special affection, and I started drifting backward, just me and President Roosevelt: how I did a big report on him in fifth grade and had to dress up like him, too; and how in college I'd go to the basement of the library when I was trying to duck my course work and go through dusty *National Geographics* from the early 1900s and flip through articles on Roosevelt and his trips to Africa, where he hunted big game. Your dad had been intrigued by him because he had belonged to Alpha Delta Phi in college like Jeremy did, and because he created the national park system and we loved camping in the parks before we were married. And I remembered Jeremy and me running through the Rockies in pouring rain with lightning hitting the cliff above us, and laughing, because that was the trip where we knew we were going to get married.

A door swung open and they brought us into another room where President Bush was. I heard maybe every tenth word, but the general message was that our family members were heroes, which was already sounding awfully familiar. Then Bush mentioned your daddy by name, and it was like another stab in the ribs reminding me that I was here because he was gone. We all lined up outside a big sitting room into which we were brought one family at a time. George and Laura Bush were there and they gave each of us a few minutes. I was second or third in line.

I approached the president and his eyes were full of tears.

He knew who I was, but he seemed overcome and couldn't get any words out. He hugged me.

Laura Bush looked at you and she said, "She is such a pretty little thing. She really looks like her daddy."

Afterward, we were taken to another room where there was a big table with tea and cookies, and there were little children running around and crawling under the table. People came up to me with odd questions, like, "So-and-so had a premonition that her husband shouldn't fly that day. Did you have any weird feelings like that?" This didn't seem to me the time to talk about this. Not that I could have reported any extrasensory early warnings. Then I spotted Lisa Beamer, whom I had met before. We chatted about her pregnancy and her children and I felt more comfortable immediately. I also met Deena Burnett, whose husband, Tom, also stormed the cockpit. She had three beautiful little girls with her, dressed identically with matching bows in their hair. I was grateful that Deena, Lisa, and I did not talk about Flight 93 at all.

On our way out, we were escorted down a long, glassed-in hall. Through one side you could see flower gardens. Dozens of White House staff were in the hall sobbing as we walked by. It was too much. I could feel this wall of sadness, sweeping through the hallway like a thunderhead, a sadness beyond hope. Some people apparently recognized me because I'd appeared on TV, and here they were offering me their hearts. I fought a kind of fluttering, drowning sensation, and I pushed all my feelings down into my fingernails and dug my fingernails into my palm as hard as I could, until I felt blood. That helped, and from then on whenever

I found myself in a similar situation, I'd use this fingernail technique, distracting panic with pain. It doesn't have an attractive ring to it, but it beats curling into a fetal ball in the middle of the White House.

The phone clanged incessantly at the Greenwood Lake house. The media and well-wishers and everyone else on the planet who needed my time were costing me the few moments of calm I had left after taking care of you. Jeremy's company had posted a notice honoring him on their Web site, but that didn't stop them from harassing me with requests to please send back Jeremy's fax machine and docking station.

"You know what? I'm all by myself with a thirteen-week-old baby," I told them when they called. "If you want it that badly, come and get it."

As Hunter Thompson, one of your daddy's favorite authors, would say, the weasels were definitely closing in.

So I did what Dr. Thompson would do—I fled, driving with my brother Pieter and his girlfriend down to Grandpa and Grandma's vacation house, in Kiawah, South Carolina. Kiawah is a golf resort, which is why Grandpa wanted to be there, though I don't care for golf myself. Kiawah has very seductive beaches, wide and white, and every day I'd walk along the ocean. The pugs had been temporarily relocated to Kiawah, so we chased them around. Eventually I'd find a quiet place and sit and talk to Daddy, and write his name in the sand. It was a confusing time. I was still struggling to figure out what the hell had happened to me. I spent hours on the beach, trying to chart a way through the day. I knew no one on the island other than my parents. I hadn't spent this much time with them since I was seventeen and before long I started to feel like the walls were closing in on me.

I did a few interviews, some for newspapers, one for a book, plus the *Oprah Winfrey Show,* which is seen by so many people that I felt it would cover all the bases for television. Talking to reporter after reporter, you repeat the same facts, tell the same stories, cry in the same places, and feel wrung out like a rag afterward. I was torn, because I didn't want to become an official 9/11 hero-widow. It's too much work, for one thing. Yet I couldn't stand the idea that what Jeremy did would be overlooked. So I did interviews, but I put limits on the number and type. I was falling apart on the morning of the Oprah interview, but her show is about people falling apart and putting themselves back together again so I was a perfect fit.

All the interviews revolved around my last phone call with Jer. That got me thinking about how shocked Jeremy had been that the terrorists had been able to board the plane with an array of weapons.

"I don't know how these people got on the plane with what they have," he told me.

One of the knives the hijackers carried was recovered from Shanksville and a picture of it showed up in a news magazine. It was a huge thing, jagged-edged, a tool for slaughter. No one should ever have been able to get on an airplane anywhere in the world with something like that. This realization launched an important evolution in my thinking. I began to understand that the Flight 93 saga was not an act of God, unforeseen and unforeseeable, but rather resulted from a failure by people at the airlines and elsewhere to carry out their primary responsibility, which was to protect the lives of the passengers.

At Kiawah, I found myself focusing compulsively on the timeline of events that morning. I couldn't help it—the chronology itself begged for further examination. The more I thought about it, the more obvious it became that there were certain questions about your daddy's flight that didn't apply to the other planes hijacked that day because so much had already happened by the 8:42 A.M. departure time of United Flight 93—the last to take off and the last to be hijacked. Before it had even turned onto the runway, American Airlines Flight 11 had been hijacked, and a message to that effect had been broadcast to air traffic controllers. Five minutes after Flight 93 took off, Flight 11 smashed into the north tower of the World Trade Center, a sight witnessed by passengers on a plane that took off immediately after Jeremy's. And it was known even before that, by 8:15 A.M., that another United flight, 175, had also been hijacked, and at 9:03 A.M. a few minutes after the first World Trade Center crash, that plane had rammed into the south tower.

Meanwhile, as is apparent both from radio broadcasts and the cockpit voice recorder, Jeremy's plane wasn't hijacked until about 9:30 A.M. For almost an hour, while all of this horror unfolded in the skies, nothing consequential was done, until 9:40, when United, under orders from the Federal Aviation Administration, directed all its planes to land immediately. That order was ignored by whoever was sitting at the controls of Flight 93, which by then had already made an unauthorized turn to the southeast, toward Washington, D.C.

It was a compelling series of clues that seemed to lead inexorably to this: alone among the hijacked aircraft, Jeremy's plane might have been saved. This thought began a long disillusioning process that would eventually lead me to consider legal action against the airlines. For now, I merely mulled at length over this chain of events.

There were other disturbing aspects to the very special situation of Flight 93. Although it had been flattering to hear President Bush express his personal gratitude for what Jeremy and the other passengers did to "save" the White House, I knew when he said it that this simply wasn't true. Vice President Dick Cheney had already admitted to reporters that the president himself had authorized fighters to shoot down Flight 93 if it continued toward Washington. By nine-thirty that morning, at least three F-16s were in the air, flying a defensive perimeter around the capital at better than 600 miles per hour, with the capability of jumping to their supersonic top speed of 1,500 miles per hour. By the time Flight 93 reached Shanksville, just 180 miles from the capital, the Air Force was no more than 10 minutes away from destroying it.

In interviews when someone lobbed what they thought was a soft question at me about whether or not I was proud that Jeremy saved the White House, they'd get a big surprise. I'd reply that I wasn't, because he didn't save it, and he didn't need to save it since it was being very ably defended by the Air Force, which in fact was preparing to blast my husband and forty other civilians out of the sky. I mentioned this to one of the people from *Dateline* and she just about fell out of her chair.

What Jeremy did do was convert a national trauma that might have been unendurable coming on top of what had already happened on September 11th into a moment of sustenance and comfort. I was proud of your daddy because he took fate into his own hands, as he always did. Just being Jeremy, he wouldn't stand for the worst result. And so he gave us this wonderful story, a national myth to elevate our grief. He didn't save the White House, but he showed us so clearly the part of the soul that stands up and says, you can take me into the ground with you, but I'll fight you, I'll bloody you, I'm bigger than you know. At some moments in history, a moral victory looms larger and becomes more important than the other kind.

I will admit that though I understand why Bush gave the shoot-down order, I was furious when I found out about it, and even more appreciative of what Jeremy and the others accomplished. Having our Air Force fire missiles at an airliner full of innocent American civilians—what an ugly thing for us all to have to live with. Had it occurred, it would certainly have made life a lot more difficult for me and the other survivors, who would then have had to stifle a very natural rage at their own government for being the proximate cause of their loved ones' deaths.

These are some of the thoughts I was thinking in Kiawah. My mind was rarely at rest. If it wasn't occupied with today, it was picking through the past, and this was the only past it was interested in.

You and I lived with Grandma and Grandpa on Kiawah Island for two months. We had Thanksgiving there, a mournful event that I remember chiefly because I ate almost nothing except two pieces of pumpkin pie—a favorite of Jeremy's—one for me, one for him. Thanksgiving was the low point, a signal that the Kiawah rest cure was over. I burned rubber to get from South Carolina to New Jersey in one day, stopping only for gas and to give you a snack. I was so excited to be going home.

Soon after I got back to the Greenwood Lake house, the doorbell rang and I found two people I didn't know standing at the door with a casserole dish. The woman said she was from across the lake and had cooked me chicken parmigiana. All I could do was weep. I said, "I'm sorry, thank you, but . . ." and closed the door on them. I felt indescribably awkward about losing it in front of strangers, people who were just trying to be kind and who undoubtedly left feeling terrible, thinking they had upset me even more. They didn't know I was crying long before they arrived.

Within a day or so of this—and this sort of breakdown was no isolated incident, but a more or less daily occurrence—I started going to a 9/11 survivors therapy group that met for an hour and a half on Wednesdays not far from Hewitt. I was already being treated by a private therapist, a very spiritual woman with whom I felt comfortable and had first seen when I suffered a miscarriage before I got pregnant with you, but I needed something else as well. I didn't normally consider myself the kind of person who would pour out her feelings to a bunch of strangers at a therapy group, but here I was, thirty-one years old, and nothing felt normal to me. The contours of my own life seemed alien. I had spent a little time with Lisa Beamer and there was an unspoken comfort there, as though I didn't need to explain things. My closest friends could offer their sympathy, but even they couldn't fathom what was going on inside of me.

The therapy group convened in a mansion with a purple door, a mental health facility inside which people were milling around doing things—I had no idea what. I walked into a room and there were couches and chairs and about a dozen women sitting in a circle with a box of tissues in the middle.

I was late. There was a short introduction by the therapist. I sat on the couch. All the women were World Trade Center survivors except me, ten widows and two mothers, give or take a couple of widows. The group included Dyan, who lost her husband in the collapse. Dyan lived quite near me and was my original contact with the group.

After the introductory chit-chat, one woman began to talk, only she couldn't talk. She started shrieking. It sent a chill up my spine. Death was in the room and this was the sound it made. Then someone else spoke and for the first time, I was seeing faces to go with the stories I'd been hearing. One woman was pregnant, one was sick, every story was worse than every other story. I stifled the impulse to leave, thinking, *Well, my story's pretty terrible, too. I do need to be here.*

And then I started to talk.

"I'm Lyz Glick, wife of Jeremy Glick, who was on Flight

93," I said. If you put a gun to my head, I could in no way remember anything else that came out of my mouth. The response was welcoming and the ice was broken. We shared stories and pictures of our men so the group could get to know them as well. Most of the victims were at the financial services companies, several at Cantor Fitzgerald. One husband had been a firefighter. Hands reached constantly into the center for that box of tissues and mine were among them.

In the early sessions, there was little response to our stories, but little was required. We were more interested in sharing resources. Who're you talking to at the Red Cross? Who did you speak to at the medical examiner's office? What have you heard? What lawyer are you seeing? Do you have someone you could recommend?

I brought you to all the early meetings. My private therapy session was also on Wednesday, and you'd sit in my lap while I talked to Helen. You'd fall asleep for your nap while I drove the half hour to the 9/11 group in New Jersey. I'd set you down in your car seat in the middle of the room and you'd sleep through the whole meeting.

We talked a lot about our children. That was one of the great attractions of the experience, for as a mother, I had felt completely, utterly alone. Dyan, my original link to the group, has a son, Dean, a couple of weeks younger than you, and most of the women have small children, ranging from two born after September 11th to two your age to a few a bit older. It was useful, though wrenching, to hear what children do at different stages. There were kids who were three who were losing the memory of their father, and a mother who wanted to know how to deal with a grieving six-year-old.

So I think, Emmy, that you were perhaps the biggest single reason for my embarking on this.

I didn't care at all for our therapist's methods at first. As the weeks rolled on, she kept coming up with these sort of gimmicks that would help us "get our feelings out another way," like role-playing and art assignments. I cringed at this kind of thing. I felt sure Jeremy would be gunning the car to get back to the lake at the first mention of role-playing. It was all mildly embarrassing.

"Okay," our therapist said one morning. "I want you to write a letter from your husband up in heaven. Think about what he would say to you, what advice he'd give you, and write it down."

My immediate reaction was, *Screw you, no way am I doing this, leave me alone,* and I wasn't the only one. The other women in the group were very much like me: college-educated, white, articulate, suburban. Most were uninhibited about speaking up, confident in their ability to handle themselves. They were all, in fact, similar to women I grew up with. We were comfortably off, and no one complained about having any economic challenges as a result of 9/11, for which we were grateful and which set us apart from others less fortunate. I think many of us felt above this kind of silly exercise.

We grumbled internally for about fifteen minutes before we started putting our pens to paper. The next thing you knew, we were bawling and scribbling. If you read our letters you'd find them almost identical, yet for each of us they produced an extraordinarily intimate emotional experience. It turned out to be quite a difficult thing to do. Mine had

Jeremy asking me to focus on my own happiness and assuring me everything was fine where he was. (I had another version where he hated heaven because it was so boring.) And he urged me to try and have a little fun.

I came to have a great deal more respect for this brand of therapy, although our counselor often seemed superfluous because we all supported each other so unreservedly and immediately. And though the exercises sounded hokey, their value became apparent when you did them. Every week, I was happy that there was this group of women who woke up in the morning just like I did saying, Oh God, what am I going to do? and went to bed at night, alone. Some of them went to other groups on Friday night. I didn't though. I became close friends with some of the group members outside of therapy. I knew I needed to be there. And the best part was, they needed me there. Here was one place in my life where I was uniquely qualified to lend strength to someone else.

One topic on which the therapy group focused was helping us make certain decisions that were probably specific to our situation. Saying no to things that felt wrong to us was a key one, and this really started to come up as we faced our first Christmas without our men. I was already getting a lot of practice in saying no, and I'm usually pretty good about taking care of myself emotionally. We discussed in some detail where we wanted to go and whom we wanted to see and where and whom we didn't.

But one experience the other women didn't quite understand the way I did was the public role of hero-widow that had been thrust upon me. Strangers from the very strangest part of the outside world kept intruding in bizarre ways. While I was still in Kiawah, a letter was forwarded from Hewitt. It was written in a stilted, semiliterate kind of handwriting. Since this was during the anthrax scare, Grandpa, Grandma and I were all a bit afraid to open it, so we took it outside before we did—as though that would make any difference if it was packed with deadly toxins. Inside was a business card with a picture of Santa and a note explaining that the sender had made up some commemorative pins he wanted to give me.

By the time I returned to New Jersey I had completely forgotten about this. Then around Christmastime, the doorbell rang. You were napping, and though I had just stepped from the shower, I was already on the phone with Grandpa. I ignored the bell, but it rang again and again, and when I looked outside, I saw a car with government plates. My first thought was it was the crash site investigators. Maybe they'd found Jeremy's wedding ring or something.

I opened the door, and there was this strange guy with a white beard, looking just like Santa, wearing a shirt with a picture of Jesus on it. He seemed to be . . . on edge.

"I wanted to give you some of these pins," he said. Then he strode past me into the living room and burst into tears.

"Can I have a hug?" he said.

Oh my god. I was standing there in my bathrobe, dripping all over the floor, stunned.

"No!" I said.

I don't think Santa ever contemplated this "no," because

the next thing I knew he was slamming the door to his car and heading back to his native land.

I think it's safe to say that the other ladies in the group did not have unbalanced strangers dressed as Santa striding into their living rooms demanding hugs. Yet each of us, in her own way, has dealt with something equally strange.

I was on the phone with a friend some time after the Santa incident and I told him about finding the videotape of Jeremy talking to you on the changing table.

"Have you gone through his desk?" he asked.

"No."

"Well, as long as you're on this grand tour of the past and looking for clues and all that, wouldn't that be a good idea?"

Jeremy's desk in the house, as opposed to his office desk, was one of those personal zones I had been fearful about rummaging through. But now I was seized with an emboldening curiosity. As soon as I hung up, I put you down for your nap and started poking around. In the top drawer, in his lefty handwriting, a chaotic jumble of loops and kinks, I found a list of goals, a kind of snapshot of Jeremy that I could date to a year before he died because of references to work he was doing on the house. "Roof stuff done," he wrote.

It was a numbered list. Some of the goals had to do with the marketing work he did for his Internet company, things he hated that he planned to force himself to do. "Three meetings, three hours cold calling per week." Like most salesmen, he loathed making "cold calls," soliciting business from companies that were essentially strangers, though he had a way of engaging people that made him unusually good at it.

He was going to force himself to go to the gym at least four times a week, to get up at 7:30 A.M., arrive at work an hour later, and to "end year on good note and take long vacation." *I'm going to need some help with that this year, Jer,* I thought.

Then: "Take care of Lyz. Get her through tough times. Take care of Lyz mentally."

That kind of restarted my ongoing conversation with him, like he'd just passed me a note in school. I told him that he'd always been there for me, and that it was overwhelming to think he'd felt he should be doing more. *Well, you were always there until now—and now look at what I'm dealing with. Maybe there's a way for you to keep helping. Nobody else seems to be able to.*

After a couple of hours of this, you woke up, and I had to say good-bye. *Talk more later, Jer. Okay? Any advice would be sincerely appreciated. Things here on earth don't seem to be getting a lot easier.*

Dorrian's Red Hand

Lyz visiting Kakadu National Park;
Australia, fall 1990

Dear Emmy,

As you can see, your daddy's college career got off to a rocky start, and it didn't improve much for quite a while. I knew little about his situation because we talked only sporadically, so much of what I'm about to tell you I found out later from his friends at college, especially Ron Zaykowski, who became Jeremy's best pal at the University of Rochester.

The Jeremy that Ron got to know was in pain. He felt disinherited by his parents and rejected by the woman he loved—he called me "the wench"—and he didn't give a damn about much of anything. Rochester had not even been his first choice—he wanted to go to Williams in Massachusetts. So Jeremy drank a lot, partied a lot, and did virtually no schoolwork, which was easy enough because at Rochester, freshman grades don't count toward the student's final average. He was going to try out for soccer but he abandoned that idea along with any kind of organized athletics. Since he was broke, he took a part-time job. Kim Bangash lent him the money to buy a motorcycle so he could get to work, an absurd choice since Rochester is located in upstate

New York and is buried in snow for much of the school year. Somehow he rode the motorcycle through slush and ice until eventually it died of natural causes.

Of course, Jeremy had no fear of riding the motorcycle. Nor was he afraid of partying past the point of physical collapse, nor of big, intimidating football players like Ron who became his close friends. Early in their friendship, Ron and Jeremy got into such a boisterous argument about whether the Giants or the Eagles was the better team that finally Jeremy told him to knock it off.

"Dude, I will mess you up," said Jeremy.

"Are you kidding?" laughed Ron, who outweighed Jeremy by 100 pounds. "I'll snap you in *half*."

"Go ahead. Give it a shot," said Jeremy.

Jeremy's eyes were still and black.

"I'll break your wrist before you even get your hand up," Jeremy said. Not that they really would have fought, but later when Ron found out about Jeremy's martial arts background, he realized it was probably best they hadn't.

Jeremy and I spent a good deal of time together the summer after freshman year. Despite our estrangement, it seemed such a natural arrangement that we couldn't stay away from each other, and we became romantically involved once again. He spent the rest of his time lifeguarding and barhopping New York City with Jimmy Best. Jimmy, who was also a lifeguard, remembers that they were so exhausted after their urban adventures that they would fall asleep in their lifeguard chairs with sunglasses hiding their closed eyes.

But when Jer was about to return to Rochester and I to

Colby for our sophomore year, I brushed off any idea of remaining romantically involved. I wanted my own life at school, and real boyfriends close at hand, rather than problematic, long-distance male companionship, despite the fact that none of my Colby boyfriends ever measured up to Jeremy. Jeremy, once again, felt jilted, dumped. He was furious and he didn't hide it. For all practical purposes, our relationship was over. Tormented that he couldn't have me, he returned to the same self-destructive path he had followed the previous year. He was rarely seen in class, but was bright enough that he managed to keep his head above water academically—just barely.

Even rugged Ron couldn't keep up with Jeremy, who seemed hell-bent on setting some kind of record for consecutive nights of inebriation and miles traveled in pursuit of beer. There was a storied trip to Clark University, in central Massachusetts, where Jeremy had a friend. The weekend was a spiral of besotted fun that began Friday night and ran into Saturday night, at which point Jeremy and Ron found themselves in a house of unknown ownership celebrating with people they had never seen before. Ron looked over at Jeremy, who hadn't slept in days. He was swaying a little. Ron thought he was kidding around. Jeremy did that a lot: He'd suddenly drop to his knees like a heart-attack victim. Or you'd hear a scream and Jeremy would come falling out of a tree. This time, his legs buckled and he fell backward flat onto a coffee table, spilling drinks all over the floor. Ron still thought it was a joke, but then everyone started running toward him. Jeremy was out cold. Ron helped carry him outside. It was unclear for a while whether an ambulance would have to be called. It scared the hell out of Ron.

Later in life, Jeremy would say to Ron, "I think I died during that period because I don't remember anything. Something happened to me."

And yet in spite of it all, Jeremy impressed not only Ron but his other classmates as the smartest person they had ever met, a young man of unlimited potential, and a leader. Ron and Jeremy were able to rent a spacious house just a block from campus based entirely on the fact that Jeremy had the landlord convinced he was a neuroscience graduate student. He spoke knowledgeably of neurotransmitters and the hemispheres of the brain and sectioning the basal ganglia. His only connection to the discipline, though, was a job caring for the gorillas and chimpanzees in the university's neurological testing lab. He thought the lab was extremely cool, and somehow managed to soak up a tremendous amount of information on the subject, which he rattled off at the landlord, who would never have rented a house to sophomores. Of course, once in possession of the house, parties could now be held on an almost continous basis.

The spring of sophomore year, Jeremy met members of the Alpha Delta Phi fraternity. He felt they were kindred spirits, and with his usual infectious enthusiasm, convinced Ron and some other friends to join, too. Behind all the hard-drinking and don't-give-a-damn attitude, Jeremy wanted to be part of something bigger. He bonded naturally with talented, ambitious people, and this was represented by Alpha Delta Phi, a fraternity known for its literary bent that had once had Francis Bellamy, author of the pledge of allegiance, and Teddy Roosevelt as brothers.

To get in, Jeremy and Ron were told they had to memorize the names of all the brothers, the history of the frat, and huge amounts of apparently meaningless blather. Jeremy wanted to belong, but as usual, he didn't want to do anything he didn't want to do, and he refused to memorize. He was the world's worst pledge. The would-be frat members would be tested on their knowledge of Alpha Delta Phi lore, and he'd make an ass out of all of them because he never knew any of the answers. Ron berated him for it, but it made no difference to Jeremy.

In the end, they were all accepted anyway, and once in, they learned that it had never been about whether they knew the correct answers, but how they handled the questioning. It had all been a test of character, and Jeremy dazzled the frat brothers with the sheer strength of his determination not to submit, *not to ever learn this nonsense no matter what they did to him.* He was so strong, such an individual, the rest of the fraternity was afraid of him. People would come up to Ron and say, "You better keep an eye on that guy. He looks like he's going to snap."

I spent that summer at Windham, while Jeremy lifeguarded in New Jersey and partied in Manhattan, just like the previous summer. He was still angry at me and I was afraid to call him, so we simply stayed away from each other.

Ron and Jeremy were officially inducted into Alpha Delta Phi in September of their junior year. Jeremy was looking forward to making a fresh start academically, and to having a kind of family at college. And then, early that fall, everything changed. There had been a series of reverses at home. His father had lost his job and the house that Jeremy grew up in and, shortly thereafter, suffered a heart attack. It was suddenly clear that there would be no money to pay for Jeremy's junior year, and Oma and Opa told Jeremy he would have to come home. Jeremy refused to accept the obvious and started attending classes even though he wasn't registered. Finally there came an ultimatum from New Jersey: You're not in school. You're not going to be. Get home. Everyone is going to have to pull together for the good of the family.

Ron had tears in his eyes. He knew Jeremy felt he was going home as a failure, to a family he believed was ashamed of him. All his worst fears had been realized.

"I'm going to come back," Jeremy promised. "We're brothers now and I'm coming back."

Jeremy moved into a room in the house his family had rented, not far from their old address in Oradell. He had several jobs, contributing some of his earnings to his parents. He was a personal trainer at a gym, and unloaded trucks at a Bloomingdale's in Hackensack. That winter, Jimmy Best came home for his vacation and they worked side by side at Bloomingdale's. Jeremy loved the writer Hunter Thompson, and he and Jimmy would move a few hundred pounds of freight, then disappear into the storage rooms of Bloomingdale's and page through *Fear and Loathing in Las Vegas,* which they would paraphrase while they worked.

"As your attorney, I advise you to get off your ass and unload this truck," Jeremy would say.

"One more word out of you and I'll rip your lungs out," Jimmy would say.

They would read passages aloud to each other, even out in the freezing cold on the loading dock, stamping their feet and giggling at the idea of Dr. Thompson hallucinating that the patrons of the hotel bar were actually huge pterodactyls stomping through puddles of fresh blood. Jeremy also talked Jimmy's ear off about the wonderful people he had connected with at his fraternity.

Jimmy and Jeremy were able to find some fun together on an exhaust-stained loading dock in midwinter, but for most of the year, Jeremy was alone and more depressed than he had ever been. I was completely out of touch with him. Jer called Ron Zaykowski at least once a week: "I'm making money. I'm going to come back." But Ron thought the odds of this were poor. Rochester was an expensive private university. He couldn't see how Jeremy could possibly earn enough money, even if he had four jobs.

Jeremy kept working. It took a lot out of him to be at home, but he accepted it, he did it. And as his stay lengthened, any damage to his very strong bonds with his parents was repaired. Jeremy had, after all, come home. He was working, he was helping, he was doing everything Oma and Opa asked. In fact, he did nothing else except to earn his wages and plan and promise himself that he would never let something like this happen to him again, that he would never be so dominated, so humbled by circumstance. Something else was happening inside of him that Ron couldn't detect, that Jimmy hadn't noticed, and that I certainly knew nothing about. But Opa and Oma could see it. Jeremy's character was toughening to match his body. He was growing up.

That year, I was preoccupied with adventures and misfortunes of my own, and was studying abroad much of the time in Australia and Africa as part of my anthropology major at Colby. I knew nothing of Jeremy's situation, nor did he know anything of mine, except that I was supposed to be out of the country. We had both been left with a sour taste upon separating just before our sophomore year, which was the low point in our history together.

The summer before my senior year, I was recuperating from some rather frightening experiences abroad, living in New York City in a studio apartment my parents kept on the Upper East Side and working as a volunteer in the ornithology department at the Museum of Natural History. My high school friend Diana Dobin came for a visit on my first weekend in the city. We had dinner near the apartment and wandered across the street for drinks, which, having turned twenty-one, we could now do legally. The place across the street was Dorrian's Red Hand, which was infamous for being the bar where Robert Chambers, the so-called Prepple Murderer, met his victim. We ran into another friend from high school there and wound up in the back of this huge, bustling place jammed with young people, a real scene.

The first question the high school friend asked was, "What's up with you and Jeremy?"

I launched into a major narration of what had happened

between us, and how I loved him and missed him, but everything was so screwed up and I knew he hated me and I couldn't call him. When I took a breath, Diana said, "C'mon. Let's go up to the bar and get another drink."

The bar was up at the front and we had no sooner reached it when Diana turned around and said, "It's Jeremy and Jim!"

I turned and ran at top speed toward the back. Jeremy saw Diana chasing after this little blond pony-tail and knew immediately it was me. I'd been wishing he would appear, and suddenly he materialized. Nevertheless the tumblers in my head were spinning in anticipation and anxiety. Before I knew it we were sitting side by side, holding hands and looking at each other as though nothing had ever been wrong. Just the most natural thing in the world, like we'd gotten up from this very spot a minute ago and now were back, picking up the conversation.

There really was a lot to say.

My junior year had started with a plane crash.

It was the end of the previous summer, one week before I was to leave for a semester of environmental field study in Australia that would tie in with my anthropology major. Almost everyone at Colby takes their junior year abroad, and my longtime roommate, Jodi Spear, was about to leave for Japan. I was shopping in Albany in preparation for my own trip. It had been a day of reminders of Jodi. At the mall, I'd seen a sun dress she'd worn that I really liked, and it made me think, "Damn, Jodi's leaving in a couple of days. Got to call her." As I drove back to Windham I heard something on the radio about the crash of a small plane near Boston, but I turned it off. I walked into the living room of our house at Windham. My mother was pale.

"Sit down, Lyzzy," she said.

"I don't want to sit down," I said. I thought, *Pieter's traveling today. Something's happened to Pieter.*

And then she told me that Jodi's plane had crashed while flying to Boston from the Spears' summer house in Cape Cod, killing Jodi, her mother, and her father, who was a pilot.

From that moment through the funeral and right up until my plane took off for Australia encompassed six days and I was awake almost the whole time. Only when the plane hit cruising altitude did I fall asleep, and I didn't wake up until we were across the Pacific.

The program was based in Cairns, in northern Queensland, a rainforest area, and our first assignment was to observe the different ecosystems of that environment. We went to the coast and did some marine biology, which amounted to scuba diving and looking at fish. The program wasn't academically challenging, which some students didn't like, but I appreciated the hands-on approach, the freedom, being out in the open. We camped in the arid outback and studied aboriginal rock art. These places were sacred to the aborigines and when you were in them, you felt poised between this world and the next, in a lunar stillness of dry rocks. I would find a big brown boulder and sit by myself, feeling close to God, though I wasn't really thinking about God in any specific way. Up on the rocks, I would have my talks with Jodi and try to rationalize things—just as I later did with your daddy.

And, as I would with Jer, I had vivid dreams about Jodi. We'd be sitting together, talking very quietly. I'd wake up feeling refreshed. The dreams didn't wipe away my fear of flying, which was unfortunate because we flew a great deal from one part of Australia to another and I cried every time I got on a plane. I'd sit next to Shari, a woman I met over there in whom I immediately felt I could confide. She was from the University of Vermont, an adventurous, humorous spirit who became a lifelong pal. We were inseparable the entire time I was in Australia.

By the end of December I was back in Maine—snowy, gray Maine. There were so many reminders of Jodi for me—and for my other roommate, Sura, who had lived with Jodi and me—that we both wound up going to the school psychotherapist. As it turned out, there wasn't much therapy involved. It just meant that once a week I went somewhere and cried for an hour.

I was determined to keep moving, because that's the only way I know to heal. My first choice for fieldwork in anthropology had always been Africa, and after the successful experience in Australia, my parents lost their fear of it and allowed me to apply for an anthropology field study program in Kenya. I was accepted and left at the end of June 1991, directly from Windham, never returning to New Jersey. I'd heard Jeremy was working and living at the Jersey shore and though I was tempted to call him, I didn't have the courage. I would regret that decision in the weeks to come.

We flew to Nairobi, stopping in Frankfurt, by which time I'd already met the other members of the group. There were eleven of us, some undergraduates, some not, ranging in ages from late teens to mid-twenties. The moment we arrived in Nairobi, things didn't go as expected. The plan was to be in the Kenyan capital a couple of days to pick up supplies and then push north, near the border with Ethiopia, where we would be studying a tribe called the Boran. Instead we sat in a run-down hostel outside of Nairobi for much of a week, jammed in one room, killing the boredom by organizing nature walks into the spectacular countryside nearby. Our academic director, a renowned ornithologist, was said to be down with malaria. He eventually showed up, an overweight little African man in his late forties with eyes bright red and bloodshot, not friendly at all. We were relieved to be getting under way.

And so we set out through Kenya, the eleven of us, our red-eyed academic director, his assistant, a paramedic, and a driver in two white vans for what we expected would be six weeks of field study. We drove through mountains on a paved road but then reached the dry, equatorial plain, where the road was dirt and very poor. The religion was Islam, and in the towns at sundown, everyone went to the mosques to sing and pray. We camped in two-person tents in game refuges and parks. We had incredible luck with wildlife. We watched lions eat a zebra. We went for a walk one day and came upon a fifteen-foot python ingesting half a gazelle.

A zipper was broken on one of the tents, and you did not want to get that one, but I got the broken tent the night of the python.

Meanwhile, a journey that was supposed to take a few days was stretching out interminably. The reason was simple—Africa. All of us had developed stomach parasites and we were always having to stop so someone could dash into a nearby clump of brush and be sick. It took two days to fix the van when it overheated, hardly a major mechanical failure in most places. Time couldn't be made up because there were bandits and it wasn't safe to drive at night. It was worse where we were heading. Ethiopia was in the throes of civil war and more than half the population were refugees.

It didn't really matter because we never got anywhere near the Boran. We were 350 miles from Nairobi when our academic director, who had taken to disappearing into local villages to get drunk, vanished altogether. We'd pitched our tents on the edge of the game preserve at Marsabit, which was surrounded by an enormous camp jammed with Ethiopians fleeing the war. We had no food, and we certainly weren't going to beg for any at the refugee camp. After four days of this, we awoke to find that our driver had absconded with the remaining van, so we walked into Marsabit where we were thrilled to find a little restaurant. I had eggs and a Fanta. I was savoring the meal when the whole world started spinning. I felt like I was going to throw up or pass out. My next memory is of being in the van. The driver was there, and I was looking out the window at the Kenyans crowding around, still feeling weak and dizzy and thinking, *just give me some space to breathe.* They took me to a health clinic and my blood test came back positive for malaria.

By the time I got back to camp, I felt better, but that night, the illness returned, with fever, sweats, and chills. Our generator broke so we didn't have light and no one could figure out how to get it working again. As morning approached, the baboons in the trees started beating their chests and screaming, which we had been told was a sign of an approaching herd of elephants. *I'm sick with malaria and we're going to be trampled by elephants,* I thought, shivering in my sleeping bag.

The next morning we had a meeting. We were all furious. Just two weeks into the program, we'd been abandoned in some godforsaken place in Africa, hungry, ill, and surrounded by starving refugees, baboons, and elephants. We decided we were going to have to get ourselves home, one way or another. The driver took us to a phone in the game preserve. All of us had signed up with the Flying Doctors in case of medical emergency, and since I was demonstrably sick, the Doctors agreed to evacuate me by air. There would be an extra seat on the plane, so Cathy, a Californian whose boyfriend lived in Nairobi, would fly out too. The others decided to join a caravan of vehicles—the only safe way to travel—that was heading back to the capital the next day.

I was to be picked up at a nearby landing strip in a few hours, so we hurried back to camp. As I packed my gear, our academic director appeared. His eyes were redder than any eyes I'd ever seen, and wild. He insisted on driving Cathy and me, and demanded we sign a form releasing him from legal liability. We refused. He seemed to accept this, and we left. As we drove, he alternated between telling us he loved Americans and screaming that we were spoiled little brats. He seemed right on the verge of a total loss of emotional control, driving much too fast, narrowly missing people along the road. I hadn't been afraid of him before. Now I realized that he was probably insane and capable of anything. Cathy kept arguing with him. I huddled silently in the back.

The airstrip was a little yellow field in the middle of nowhere, and suddenly it sank in that in such a place, we could disappear from the face of the earth and nobody would know. But the academic director dropped off our bags and drove off. *Yes!* I thought. *Now get us out of here.* We sat on a clump of boulders. There were no buildings, no trees, no shelter of any kind from the scorching sun. We'd been there about forty minutes when the director returned, this time with a big Kenyan carrying a submachine gun. They got out, and the director was trying to split us up, insisting that Cathy go back with him to get the paramedic. My legs were shaking, but I told him I was getting on that plane and that he should leave Cathy alone, she wanted to fly out too. Both of us laughed nervously at him when he again ordered us to sign the legal release form. No way, we said. Then the big Kenyan pointed his gun at my head and we signed.

The little plane touched down and I've never been so happy to see somebody in all my life. We sat on the landing strip for another hour waiting for another vehicle to arrive because there was a critically ill man already on the plane and the academic director refused to drive him to a nearby hospital.

On the plane, they checked my vital signs and my pulse was 140 beats per minute, like I'd just ran a marathon. The on-board paramedic was concerned.

I laughed a little hysterically.

"No, it's okay. I'm actually feeling much better," I said. "I just had a kind of stressful experience."

After a brief hospital stay, I was expertly nursed by the family of Cathy's boyfriend at their house in Nairobi. I took baths and ate pizza and watched documentaries on lions. I called my folks and told them what had happened and that I was okay, and I called the field study program, which belittled my story. After a few days, I got on an airplane and flew home. I was down to ninety pounds, but was otherwise on the mend.

As I sat with Jeremy in Dorrian's Red Hand at the end of that terrible summer, I told him I'd thought of him many times in Africa, and of little else on the flight home.

"I can't believe you're here," I said over and over again as he clasped my hand. "I thought you hated me."

"How could I hate you?" he said. "You're my best friend."

It was an encounter on two levels. One level was this impossibly compressed exchange of information. "Well what's been happening with you?" "Oh, my roommate died in a plane crash and then I got malaria in Africa and my teacher held an AK-47 to my head so I wouldn't sue him and I was medevaced out of the bush by the Flying Doctors. What about you?" "Uh, my family sort of disinherited me but then my father had a heart attack and we lost our house and I had to drop out of school and come home and help them but now everything is fine with my folks and I've earned enough money to go back."

The other level is harder to put your finger on. We were again in each other's orbit. And it was just so comfortable— in a word, it felt preordained. I had grown up a little after the multiple ordeals of the past year, and I could see Jeremy wasn't a boy anymore. His anger had been replaced by a deep resolve about what he wanted to be, and what he would no longer accept from himself or from the world. And right there, I think, we fell in love all over again.

We stayed out late that night and walked the streets of Manhattan. We ended by kissing on the steps of the Metropolitan Museum of Art, after which I walked back to my apartment and he drove back to New Jersey. We saw a lot of each other over the next month before I returned for my senior and Jeremy for his long-delayed junior year. And although our parting was sad, there was no bitterness. We would again be leading separate lives at school, with no promises for the future, but Jeremy seemed to understand that it had to be that way. Because who knew what might happen in the future? Of course, now I know he had no intention of letting me get away again.

At the end of the summer, Jeremy sat down with the dean at the University of Rochester and worked out a way that he could pay his tuition and re-enroll. He was back, and no one was more surprised or delighted than Ron Zaykowski. Ron was struck by the changes in his friend. He wasn't drinking or smoking and arose bright and early for morning classes. He was a philosophy and English major who was about to work his way onto the dean's list. And he was the acknowledged leader of Alpha Delta Phi, and would soon be its president.

"Where's Jeremy Glick and who are you?" Ron would joke with him. Jer looked different, too. All the lifting and hauling and weight training of the previous year had bulked him up to 200 pounds, none of it soft. He finally had the brute power to match his skills in judo and wrestling.

I graduated that summer, moved to San Francisco, and started working. Your daddy had another year to go, but we talked on the phone regularly. He was still living the student life. I was a bit envious that he could call me at three in the morning after coming back from a Grateful Dead show while I was slaving for a recycled paper company for eight dollars an hour. By the spring I'd had enough poorly paying jobs to convince me that I should go to grad school and get my master's in anthropology.

What I didn't know was that Jeremy had been through one other critical experience during his year off from college, one he didn't mention but was thinking about now.

It had happened while Kim Bangash was visiting Jeremy in New Jersey. Jer had heard about an open invitational judo competition and Kim accompanied him there. Jeremy easily won his matches, but the competition was not of a very high caliber so it didn't mean very much. Except that there was one very big, very skillful judoka named Steve, who according to the scuttlebutt in the gym was some sort of a national power in the sport.

Jeremy had been out of competitive judo for years, so no one knew who he was, least of all Steve, who probably thought he was just going to blow by this considerably smaller opponent. Kim helped Jeremy warm up, and Jeremy went out and soundly defeated Steve, which shocked the whole gym, including Kim, who found himself thinking that Jer had skills in judo far beyond what he'd given him credit for.

Afterward, people came up to Kim and said, "Who's your friend? That guy he beat is no slouch."

"Yeah, we know that," said Kim.

Ever since then, Jeremy had been thinking about taking his judo to the next level. During his senior year, he told Ron he wanted to "make his mark" in national competition, possibly even go to the Olympics, and that spring, he started training at the University of Rochester as hard as he could. I didn't know any of this. Nor did I know that, as it happened, the national collegiate judo competition would be held in San Francisco that year.

Your daddy always seemed to have a plan, Emmy, but he often kept it a secret. In retrospect you couldn't untangle the plan from the *glick,* the luck on which he always seemed able to rely. He'd righted himself, worked his way back into school and returned to the martial arts. Yet at the end of it all there was this strange coincidence, with the judo competition scheduled for San Francisco during the year I lived there, which happened to be the final year he could have competed, so that it was almost as though someone was deliberately leaving open a door for him leading back into my life, and saying, *go ahead, kid, take a shot.*

Search Parties

Lyz carrying Olympic torch into
Times Square, December 2001

Dear Emmy,

I was seated next to a couple of Afghani women at the White House when I went for the second time a couple of weeks before Christmas. It was the three-month anniversary of September 11th, and I was accompanied by Jeremy's family. We were a somewhat odd collection, with the September 11th families and then these very nice Afghani teachers who were there to dramatize the plight of education-deprived women under the Taliban. And it was around this time, too, that some of the political fallout from 9/11 started to rain down on my therapy group. The war in Afghanistan was in the news. Opinions were strong in the group about the Arab world, and tended toward the harshly negative.

"We should just round them all up and ship them out of the country. Anyone that should be here can prove their way back in," one woman said.

I told the group about my Afghani women, and that although I knew politics brought them to the White House, it didn't matter, because I enjoyed talking to them and they were charming and seemed genuine.

"Most Muslims don't want to blow up America," I said, expressing what I thought was the obvious. "You can't look at a sizable part of the world and see it as a bunch of terrorists."

Mine was definitely the minority opinion. My politics are personal. I don't hate people in groups, just the specific individuals who did this to my husband. And I was taught to listen when someone speaks in friendship, no matter their reputation or country of origin. I have no idea, however, what the experience of being killed by Islamic men might have had on Jeremy's views. He always had the most broadranging tastes in people, irrespective of accidents of religion or geography. Kim Bangash was his best friend, and Kim is half-Pakistani. Nor was Jer homophobic—he had weight-lifting buddies at the gym who were gay.

When the Glick kids were little, there was a young woman named Virginia who went to the same swimming pool in Oradell. Virginia was perhaps nineteen years old, a little slow and not shy. She'd stride up and park herself in front of one of the children.

"You're Jeremy," Virginia would say. "Your birthday is September third, nineteen-seventy. You're ten years old."

"Right, Virginia," Jeremy would say. If it was Jared or Jennifer, it was the same conversation with different numbers. Virginia could remember them, though little else.

"You're September third, nineteen-seventy."

"That's right, Virginia. I like your bathing suit. 'Bye, Virginia," Jeremy would say.

"Good-bye, Jeremy."

It was not by chance that the Glick kids were the only

ones who didn't flee at Virginia's approach. "Talk to Virginia," Oma Glick told them. "Treat her like anyone else."

Now the borders of acceptance seemed to be shrinking, certainly in my therapy group. But the image of the tolerant Jeremy I knew is still bright in my mind, so I try not to speculate about the impact on him of one anarchic morning in September. And I think I do understand something of his state of mind at the end, because I was talking to him until three minutes before his death.

At the time of my second White House visit, outsiders couldn't get a tour of the White House due to security concerns, but as special guests we were taken through all the Christmas rooms, past a three-foot-high gingerbread replica of the White House, which, being gingerbread, was actually more like the Brown House. And that was only one of several large gingerbread houses. A lot of time and expense had gone into getting the White House ready for Christmas. There were dozens of Christmas trees, some creamed over in fake snow and hung with white fairy lights, others done in colors; and every room was decorated with holly, stockings, figurines, and wreaths.

We entered a small white ballroom. The President of the United States strode in briskly and once again gave a short speech to a small room in which I sat with you in my lap. He mentioned Jeremy, which hit me with the jolt of pain I always feel when someone speaks his name at an official occasion. To avoid another tear-stained blouse, my eyes focused on a line of foreign flags behind the podium that partially obscured a soaring Christmas tree. I found myself thinking, *Why is the Israeli flag exactly in the center, directly behind the president?* I pondered the arrangement for some time, until the speech was over.

It was a quick trip to Washington, in and out in a couple of days. Christmas was approaching, but little joy did it promise. Rather it seemed pregnant with opportunities for melancholy because Jeremy, the Jewish kid, *adored* Christmas. Jeremy loved getting presents—he really couldn't stand it if he saw something under the tree he thought was for him and it turned out to be for someone else. Christmas just beat the living tar out of Chanukah for loot. We still celebrated the Jewish holidays with his parents, but Jer looked forward to doing all the Christmas rituals with me. He'd set up the tree with my dad, and we'd trim, put up stockings. Now I dreaded those rituals, the hollow shell of an occasion with nothing inside. And you were still too little to be my Christmas co-conspirator.

One good thing did happen just before Christmas. The Olympic Committee had called while I was still in Kiawah to ask if I would run the Olympic torch into New York City for the Winter Games. I had immediately become excited at the idea, because Jer and I were enthusiastic athletes who'd talked about going skiing in Utah and then seeing some of the Olympics in Salt Lake City.

Then a dark cloud passed over me.

"Wait a minute," I said. "How far do I have to run?"

The truth was, I hadn't had any significant exercise since well before you were born. I had a vision of a mass of protoplasm laboring down Broadway while loved ones averted their eyes. A national disgrace.

"It's no marathon. Maybe two tenths of a mile," they said.

I was bathed in relief. Despite my condition, I could run two tenths of a mile—maybe even look good doing it.

"Love to," I said.

My training consisted of doing nothing. I ate donuts. I may have taken walks. But I was fully charged when the evening of the run arrived. And I think that was a turning point for me, because as I pumped into Times Square two days before Christmas and handed off the torch (which by the way, is heavier than it looks), I felt the first little spark of *me* return. The feeling was close to the one I'd get when Jeremy and I mountain-biked or ran or especially when we skiied together. I'd be motoring down the slope with Jeremy tacking ahead, hopping off moguls, but never allowing too much distance to get between us, letting me come abreast, then pulling away to launch a colossal jump from an ice cliff dangerously close to the tree line, landing and smashing on the brakes in time to swivel his head around at me and grin crookedly in the mountain sunshine.

"Niiiice," he'd say.

For the seven minutes of my Olympic appearance, I was Lyzzy again, even if the whole world had gone to hell. On TV, I might have looked like a symbol of something—of the Olympics, or maybe of a national determination to go on. I might have represented a lot of different ideas to different people because I was the widow of Jeremy Glick and I was running with a torch. But I didn't think of it that way. I was experiencing a pure catharsis that came from running before what I knew were millions of people, which for some reason triggered this sense of being cleansed. For seven glorious minutes, my demons were compelled to shut up.

———

Other than the trip to Washington, it was just you and me, Emmy, at the Greenwood Lake house between Kiawah and Christmas. You had started rolling over, so some nights I'd transfer you to a portable crib at the foot of my bed in which you seemed to like to nest. Over the several months from winter to spring, you began to develop critical attachments to certain words and objects, early stirrings of your personality. A grade school friend with whom I'd long been out of touch found me after Jeremy died and gave you Blue Dog, a kind of blanket dog with a fluffy head and flat body, and Blue Dog had to be in bed with you every night. Then there was Nah, your stuffed cat, named after the sound you thought cats made. Perhaps because other people had cats but we didn't, you developed a feline obsession. Oma and Opa still had Floyd, Jeremy's cat from college, whom you enjoyed visiting on their porch, although Floyd was so old and decrepit he was a little frightening. Eventually, your mania extended to forty books on cats, numerous cat puzzles, a height chart shaped like a cat, and the fact that you would, on occasion, meow yourself to sleep.

Most of that would come later. Your most salient characteristic right at present was that you were a handful. I was still up every night diapering and feeding and comforting you, with the only relief coming in sleepover visits by friends like Diana Dobin and Shari Solomon, who'd insist on taking over while I collapsed on my bed like a sack of laundry and slept until someone woke me up.

I needed some more permanent help with you, and I was

ready for some adult companionship. I had put aside money
for an au pair, and I started looking for one toward the end
of the year. For some reason, the agency kept sending me
applications from Middle Eastern women. Now here I have
to make a confession. I did not want a Middle Eastern
nanny, despite my fellow feeling for the Afghani women. I
simply hadn't evolved far enough to handle the idea of having an Islamic woman in my home helping to raise my
daughter. I plead guilty to that. So I kept rejecting them.

After several rejections, I finally had to say something.

"You do know who I am?"

"Oh, yes, of course," the woman said. "But we ask our
host families to be open-minded."

"You know, I have a degree in anthropology, I've traveled
around the world, I'm way more open-minded than most,
but this is just not going to happen," I said.

In the meantime, we passed Christmas at Windham with
Grandma and Grandpa and Shari. I gave myself a pair of
skis, because Jeremy had been planning to buy me new ones
for Christmas. We had filet mignon for dinner, his favorite,
and when I saw it on my plate, I asked Shari to take you for
the night, excused myself, got up from the table, and went
upstairs. I shut the door to the bedroom, turned out the
light, and gazed at a million things that flashed on the dark-
ened wall. I'd passed from celebrating the holiday, which
was impossible, to marking it with my tears. Was I sinking
or buried? Those seemed to be the alternatives.

I awoke the next morning with none of that feeling still
with me. Terror at night, relief by morning, blues in the
afternoon. Life went on in this kind of trough-and-swell

pattern through the New Year. The ups were never far from the downs and all of it seems now, looking back, to blend into a single blurry constellation of lost moments.

It may sound odd, but what roused me from this shadow life was my growing fascination with the plane crash itself.

It began with a psychic.

Emmy, you know I don't believe in the occult. I don't see auras and I don't treat my headaches with crystals. And notwithstanding the conversations I have with Jeremy, I've never believed in ESP or out-of-body experiences, and neither did Jer. But my 9/11 therapy group had become deeply enamored with psychics. Everyone in the group went to them and psychic consultations were sometimes provided free to 9/11 survivors. They were even invited to one of our parties. Eventually, despite considerable natural skepticism, I went to one in New York. Here was a woman who claimed she could bring me news from the dimension into which my husband had vanished. I could dismiss that as impossible, or I could go see her. Why would I take a chance on being wrong?

My psychic had a doctorate in psychology and was quite prominent in her field. She did her consultations from a skyscraper on Park Avenue, near Grand Central Station. Her receptionist waved me into a spare, executive-style office, done in pastel browns with a big window. Lauren was a soothing presence, wore flowing, billowy clothing, had a soft but energetic voice, was magnetic and warm. We sat across from each other.

Though I'd only given her my first name, she told me she recognized me from my TV appearances, and knew I had come to try to connect with Jeremy. I was extremely nervous. While in the waiting room, I'd briefly considered fleeing.

"Relax," she said. Then she closed her eyes and meditated a little, breathing in and out, slowly and deeply.

She looked at a point somewhere between my forehead and the wall and said, "You're going to write a book."

I had just started thinking about a book, though I had taken no concrete steps in that direction, nor had I imagined it as a series of letters to you. My first thought was that since she knew who I was, she could easily figure I had a much higher-than-average shot at writing a memoir.

We went on to something else, but then she said, "You know, there's something about letters. Do you have all these e-mail letters or—"

"Well, people have sent me letters."

"No, it's not that," she said. "It's letters that have to do with the book. Maybe you're going to have letters in the book."

She dangled some tantalizing bits and pieces in front of me. She kept mentioning someone with the initial *K,* then said it was Kim, and that Kim was a man. It happened that Kim Bangash and his wife Monica were watching you while I was in New York. She talked about "personal effects," a phrase I'd never heard, and said my husband's wedding ring, which I'd been silently hoping would turn up at the crash site, would never be found. To hear someone say that, even on such slim authority, was devastating.

Toward the end, as we started talking about the crash itself, I became emotional.

"I want to know, is Jeremy at peace? Because people are always telling me he's at peace, but I don't feel like he's at peace. Maybe because I don't feel it myself. I mean, no one is less at peace than I am," I said.

Lauren kind of went blank. She more or less stopped doing anything, almost like she didn't breathe for a couple of minutes. Then a half-smile.

"He's telling me that he has an awareness that he didn't have before, like he's been moved around like a pawn on a chessboard," she said.

I walked down Park Avenue to my car feeling a bit stunned. Our Little Man, the guy who was pushing me and Jeremy around on the chessboard! That dummy who couldn't do anything right. Somehow she'd hit on a routine Jeremy and I'd been doing since we were eighteen.

I drove back to the Bangashes in New Jersey not so much sold on psychics as feeling that somehow this woman had given me a kind of information, and that it had come from somewhere. It seemed that Lauren believed, as I did, that Jer was in a *place*. She validated certain ideas I already held but didn't fully understand, things I probably needed to believe. Things which, in any event, I did believe.

I fed you and then sat down to eat a pizza with Kim and Monica and their two little ones. Monica had lost her parents when she was quite young. It was she who told me to get out of bed quickly and to always keep moving. Monica thought psychics could be useful, if taken with a grain of salt, and she was keenly interested in my encounter.

"The weirdest thing she said was this thing about teeth," I told them.

A strange expression came over Kim's face.

"What about teeth?" he said.

"She said, 'Jeremy's showing me his teeth.' Then she asked me, 'What is it about teeth?' And I told her how we sent the dental records. And she said, 'All you're getting back is teeth.'"

Kim just about dropped his fork.

"Oh man," he said. "Nobody wanted to tell you this, but she's right on the money."

Kim explained how six months earlier, during our September visit to the crash site, the coroner had told him and Grandpa that Jeremy had been identified from teeth.

I pressed Kim for details. Teeth—meaning more than one? Which teeth? Where were they found? He didn't know. I'd have to ask the coroner.

I was surprised at my own curiosity. I found myself looking forward to a meeting between the Flight 93 families and the coroner that was to take place in a few weeks, on February 23rd. On Valentine's Day, I drove to Lisa Beamer's house in Cranbury, an hour and a half south, in central New Jersey. Lisa and I figured that since our husbands were spending Valentine's Day together, we might as well too. There was nothing very extraordinary about our Valentine's lunch, except that a few minutes of it were filmed by a television crew doing a show on Lisa who seemed absolutely fascinated that we were together on Valentine's Day.

I didn't know Lisa terribly well, but being with her always felt natural, like two old girlfriends getting together. Nine days later, I sat between her and Oma Glick when we gathered with relatives of the thirty-eight other passengers on Flight 93 at the Hilton in Woodbridge, New Jersey, to meet with Wallace Miller, the coroner of Somerset County, Pennsylvania, which was where the plane went down. We were in a kind of seminar room along with the FBI, United Way, and the owner of one of the properties that comprised the area of the crash.

We were to learn for the first time just what had been found during the search there, a vast project led by two hundred and fifty FBI investigators backed up by hundreds of technicians, excavators, professional tree climbers, volunteer searchers, and eighteen dentists who came to identify the teeth of victims.

Wally Miller was at the front of the room, a dark-haired, bony-framed guy with glasses in his mid-forties. He narrated a slide show that showed the crater, the nearby woods, and the drainage pond where one largely intact jet engine splashed down. The search had amounted to a sort of archaeological dig. The investigators burrowed down into the scorched hole into which the fuselage had disappeared, but they also fanned out to map the farthest points that material from the plane had been flung. The distribution of remains, which were found over an area of 100 acres, was not necessarily logical. A little bit of a person might turn up at the mouth of the hole. Then, a half-mile away, a little more of that person would be found. Extraordinary pains were taken to reclaim everything savable, but most of the plane and its occupants had been burned into a hot dust that dissipated through the air. Wally Miller called it "a cremation process."

I was mightily struck at hearing those words, because Lauren had used exactly the same terms. *Maybe she's just an expert on plane crashes,* I thought.

However, many kinds of "material" were recovered. Human remains and aviation parts and chunks of luggage and scraps of clothing. Hemlocks, tall, stately evergreens, grew throughout the crash site. Many were burnt like matchsticks by a fireball that rolled out of the broken neck of the aircraft when it hit. With the fireball came pieces of metal that shot into the woods. Some were found embedded six inches deep in trees. The change of season from summer to fall brought debris, including substantial pieces of aircraft and small parts of human bodies, sprinkling down gradually from hundreds of fir trees. Later, climbers were brought in to further harvest the trees.

The speed of the plane upon impact was almost unprecedented in commercial air crashes. Planes usually crash during takeoffs or landings, or while the pilot is fighting to get the craft up or down during an onboard emergency, all situations in which the aircraft travels at a reduced speed. Flight 93 came in steep and fast. The only similar instance recently was the EgyptAir disaster in which the copilot deliberately dived the plane into the Atlantic Ocean. So Flight 93 produced very little in the way of remains, even by the standards of plane crashes. Eight percent: That was how much of the bodies were recovered. Usually, said Miller, you could count on anywhere from 17 to 30 percent.

There were a lot of numbers that morning in Woodbridge, the majority of them grim. Even DNA was of no use in identifying most of the 1,500 samples of human material that were found because they were in such poor condition. However, enough matches were made so that in combination with dental records and a few fingerprints, all forty passengers were positively identified.

When Miller mentioned that remains of the four hijackers had also been located, some people got angry.

"Can you burn them?" one woman asked Miller.

"Yeah, we don't want them in there," someone else said.

Wallace said that was up to the FBI. Then he went on to more numbers.

I listened to all this in horrified fascination. Back in September, I couldn't look—now I couldn't look away. *My God, I'm sitting here listening to all this gore,* I thought, and once had to run to the bathroom after hearing a little too much. Later, instead of the bathroom, I fled to the day-care room and stared at you, sound asleep as you usually were at this time. But I kept going back to hear Wally Miller.

When Miller finished describing how the crater had been excavated, and how the vast footprint of the crash had been sectioned off and searched—by men and women advancing shoulder-to-shoulder on hands and knees—the meeting was opened up for questions.

I stood up and berated the FBI, which had issued a memo over Director Robert Mueller's signature telling us we couldn't hear the black-box recorder from the flight cabin. It was common knowledge by then that the cockpit recorder had picked up a commotion at the front of the plane just before the tape ended, capturing what sounded very much like a group of people bursting into the flight deck area.

"You're telling us we can't listen to this because it's too terrible a thing for the families to hear," I said. "Where does the FBI get the right to judge that? I can tell you that everything terrible that could happen to me has already happened. The terrible thing was losing my husband and having to live with it."

I was really furious. I had let the FBI interview me at length in the days immediately after I lost Jeremy when I least wanted to talk to anyone. I'd had them into my home. I'd reviewed with them in slow motion the most painful conversation of my life. Now I was asking for *their* help. If Jeremy was on the tape, I wanted to hear it. I was going to hear it.

People applauded. It was the first time all the families had sat together in one room for something that wasn't a ceremonial occasion, and it liberated a certain sense of power among us. Other people spoke up, agreeing with me. Deena Burnett, who lost her husband, Tom, was already lobbying hard for us to be able to listen to the black-box recording.

The FBI always appeared in groups, usually in blue suits. They made an effort at seeming sympathetic, but were clearly not the decision makers. We knew that someone in Washington would make this call. Someone we'd probably never meet.

"We hear you. It will be seriously considered," an FBI supervisor said.

I had driven to Woodbridge with Oma Glick, which had seemed like a great idea, but I dreaded having to console someone all the way back. But Oma was calm and it was I who was floundering emotionally. She spoke soothingly, and seemed to know exactly when to stop. I focused on the highway and tried to get my mind around what I'd heard. I was in a kind of twilight place where I could hear Wally Miller's voice, talking endlessly about all the things that fell out of the trees.

The deeper I went into the story of United Flight 93, the more I came to see it as a terrible, unnecessary waste of human life, which, because it occurred so late in the cycle of events that morning, was the only potentially reversible tragedy of September 11th. Around the time of the Woodbridge survivors' meeting, a local lawyer advised me that time was running out, and if I wanted to preserve my legal rights, I'd better go out and get a lawyer. And not just any lawyer, but a plaintiff's lawyer specializing in suing the airlines. I met with a number of attorneys, all of whom seemed expert, but I found myself most comfortable with Mitch Baumeister, who had left Kreindler & Kreindler, a leading aviation law firm, and gone off on his own.

Baumeister came up to Greenwood Lake and spent an afternoon with you and me, which in and of itself meant a lot. Kim Bangash was there too, because Kim acts as my financial and legal adviser, a role Jer had told Kim he wanted him to play if anything happened to him.

Baumeister was a tall, thin, bespectacled man in his early fifties. He was blunt and quite emotional about the crash. I found both qualities attractive. He said he'd filed a number of cases relating to September 11th. In one he was suing the terrorists directly and asked if I wanted in.

"I'd like to be part of it, but I'm kind of nervous about more media exposure," I said.

"How's this—when we sue, we stick your file right in the middle with all the others, so it won't be obvious," he said.

"Tricky," I laughed.

Another possibility was to sue United Airlines for negligently allowing the terrorists to get on board with weapons and failing to recall the plane during an evident spate of hijackings, among other things. The situation was complicated, however, by the fact that there was also a Victim Compensation Fund which was supposed to take care of all the 9/11 families, though no one seemed to know exactly what that meant in monetary terms or when it would happen. As far as providing some financial security for you and me, Baumeister said we would have to wait and see whether the Victim Compensation Fund would provide an adequate settlement, because those who accepted money from the fund were precluded from suing for damages. And some cases against United would undoubtedly go forward no matter what happened with the fund, which would help get to the bottom of what happened that morning.

"What's the bottom line, do you think? What will all these lawsuits prove?" I asked.

"Your husband's plane never should have taken off," he said. "But you knew that already, didn't you, Lyz?"

After your daddy died, I started dreaming differently. I continued to have regular dreams with people and creatures who talked and did things. But sometimes, I had—and still have—another kind, in which sometimes there are no distinct images. These are like an experience you can't describe afterward. You wake up and, boom, you have information and everything is very clear.

Sometime after the meeting in Woodbridge, I had one of these dreams, although this one was very visual. I didn't even know I'd had it until two days later, when I was sitting in the living room reading something in a magazine about the hijackers that sparked it off. I went, *Whoa, what about that dream I had two nights ago?*

It grew out of something I'd thought about occasionally since the Woodbridge meeting, which was that although all the passengers who described the terrorists said there were three hijackers, four boarded the aircraft and four sets of remains were found. In my dream, Jeremy is pointing to a piece of blue cloth with some orange on it, part of an aircraft seat. He's standing in the first-class cabin, just behind the cockpit, saying, "Look around the corner. Look around the corner." I can see there's a little nook between first class and the cockpit that's large enough for a person to stand in.

When I called my dad to tell him, he said he had dreamed about Jeremy the same night. In his dream, Jeremy showed him other places targeted by the terrorists—a dam and a nuclear plant. Then Kim told me he too dreamed that night of being shown things by Jeremy.

A few weeks after the dream, at around four in the morning, one of your little musical toys started playing itself for no apparent reason, so that I was awakened by the sound of a violin, your daddy's instrument, in the middle of the night. It wouldn't stop until I tore it open and yanked out the batteries.

I called Kim the next day.

"Your kids have lots of toys—do they ever just go off in your house?" I said.

Kim laughed. He had no unexplained toy phenomena to report. Dreams came up frequently in my therapy group, with some of the women saying they never had the comfort of seeing their husband walking and talking in a dream, but no one ever mentioned toys. Then it happened again when my friend Ana San Juan was visiting. We were sitting on the porch when we both heard a violin playing a few notes of Mozart.

"What is happening in your house?" she said.

I shrugged.

"I'm not even going in there," I said.

So now I started thinking about Wally Miller, the FBI, Lauren, the psychic, my dreams—all of it simply different kinds of information, scattered like debris around this big archaeological dig. And here comes our search party, Emmy, homing in on Daddy's violin, playing through a broken toy in the middle of the night.

Monkeys, Sharks, and Dragons: A Love Story

Rocky Mountain National Park, Estes Park,
Colorado, 1995

Dear Emmy,

I got an excited call from Jeremy one night in the spring of 1993, telling me he'd be competing in the National Collegiate Judo Championships in three weeks. I'd just taken my entrance exams for anthropology graduate school. I knew he had returned to judo, but I also knew that judo at Rochester was merely a club sport, a small group of people who sparred together but didn't compete against other schools. It wasn't the kind of serious program that would send someone to the nationals. Later I would discover that he had been training for much of the school year, making a lengthy round-trip from Rochester to northern New York state to work with a very skillful judoka with whom Jeremy had attended judo camp as a little boy.

With Jeremy, there was always a bit of mystery attached. He liked surprises. The championships would be held at San Francisco City College.

"You can stay with me," I told him.

"Nice," he said.

It would be the first time I'd seen him since Christmas,

but there'd been a steady patter of phone calls. Once he called and as soon as I picked up the phone, he said, "I love you I love you I love you I love you I love you . . ." Jeremy wasn't shy.

The judo championship was held in a large gym and I sat in the first row of bleachers, which were full. Practically all the competitors belonged to teams, mostly well-financed squads from colleges and universities. One was an Army group from West Point that, as it turned out, was coached by Sensei Ogasawara, Jeremy's old teacher from New Jersey.

Jeremy ran the length of the gym and jumped into Sensei's arms. Sensei was delighted to see Jeremy, who was competing as a brown belt, since he had never bothered to test for the black belt.

"Who is your coach? Where is your team?" asked Sensei.

"I don't have a coach. I don't have a team. I'm here by myself," said Jeremy.

This didn't bode well for Jeremy's chances in the tournament. Sensei agreed to help Jeremy prepare as best he could in the few hours before the preliminary matches began. In spite of his disadvantages, Jer won the three early bouts, and surprised everyone—except himself—by advancing to the final, in which he would fight a senior from Fresno State, a world-class talent who was the son of one of the greatest judo champions in Japan and had been trained by his father since childhood. Matched against him was an obscure guy named Jeremy Glick, who had only gotten back into judo a few months earlier after a five-year hiatus.

Jeremy came out in his *gi,* his white judo robe. If you'd looked under the *gi* you would have seen a skin-covered fighting machine. Broad shoulders over carved pectorals, a capacious chest supported by the narrow column of his abdomen and waist and hips. There was a precision of definition about the muscles of his forearms that powered his grip, like they'd been banged into shape with a ball-peen hammer. His legs were long and almost olive under his white uniform pants.

Around his waist was a brown obi, or belt, meaning he was ranked a brown belt, an inferior grade to the black belt held by the Fresno State kid. Jer and his competitor bowed, the referee shouted *hajime,* and they started fighting. I realized I'd never actually seen your daddy in a judo match, I'd only watched him practice. His opponent was skillful. To execute a flip, the judoka must break the opponent's balance, then get into the proper position for the throw. The Fresno State judoka broke Jeremy's balance a couple of times in the early going, but each time, Jer worked his way out. Jer counterattacked, and pulled the judoka down, but his body barreled over onto Jeremy's head. The ref shouted. They stood up. Jer rubbed his temple.

I could feel the blood beating in my throat. I didn't think I could stand watching Jer get hurt. I'd forgotten, if I ever knew, how violent the sport is. Judo means "the gentle way" but there is nothing gentle about a pair of 180-pound men trying to hurl each other onto the floor, preferably from shoulder height or better.

The ref shouted again and they resumed fighting. Jeremy seemed emboldened. You felt like he was stalking the Fresno State kid, probing for weaknesses. I didn't actually notice Jeremy sneaking his leg between the judoka's, but

I saw the kid flip over Jer's hip and land with a surprised grunt on his back. The crowd exploded in shouts. Sensei clutched his sides.

"*Wazami,*" the official yelled. Jeremy had been awarded a half point by sweeping the Fresno State kid's leg out from under him. If he could hold onto that lead for the rest of the five-minute match he would win. If his opponent got a half point, it would be a draw, and if either of them reached one full point, the match would end immediately.

This was a dangerous moment. Because the margin between defeat and victory is often just one well-executed throw, many judoka choke in this situation, trying to avoid defeat rather than seize victory, a fatal error in a sport in which a fighter who dodges his opponent is automatically disqualified. Jeremy now had to get through almost three minutes of the match without being flipped by a competitor known for brilliant throwing technique who had been virtually raised in a judo school.

Sensei shouted encouragement, prodding him to attack. The two opponents circled each other, grabbed for each other's *gi*s. It went back and forth, bodies colliding, elbows trying to wrap around necks, feet snaking between legs, a subtle change in the inclination of hips signaling where force would next be applied. Each tried to be aware of the position of the other man's obi, his belt, the center of gravity. The head, the hands, the legs could make a feint that would put the opponent off balance for the decisive fraction of a second necessary to slap on a move. So you watch the obi, because the center never lies.

I don't remember much of what happened during those

three minutes, but I knew it was up when the referee raised his hands, stepped toward the middle of the gym, and shouted, *"Soremade!"*

The fighters returned to their original positions and stood at attention, panting.

"Yusei-gachi!" the ref shouted, and pointed at Jeremy.

People went mad. They stood and stomped on the bleachers and bayed and bleated. The entire gym was ringing like the inside of a church bell. I was screaming. Jeremy walked over and shook the other judoka's hand. We were later told the Fresno State kid's right arm had been broken during the match.

It was a major upset of a black belt by a brown belt. And by a completely unknown brown belt who had neither team nor coach. Jer not only won the title of college judo champion, his skills were of such an obviously high caliber that they made him a black belt on the spot. We had to be there for some time while the officials sorted it all out. By the time we headed back to my little flat in the Haight, Jer had on his big crooked smile. Here he had this enormous talent, and it was finally being recognized as the truly formidable thing that it was. I told Jer that I was amazed, that it was a pure rush to watch him in the exercise of what can only be described as his art form.

My two roommates were away, so we had the apartment to ourselves. Jer showered and we tended to the mat burns that were all over him, and to his fingers, which had been jammed. We lit candles and put pillows on the rug in the living room and stayed up all night watching TV and talking. Across the street from our railroad flat was a halfway house. We watched that for a while from one of the windows. Sometimes you can see people fighting over there, I told Jeremy. Oh great, he said.

We didn't have very long. I find I keep saying that, but now that I look at it, we just never did. He flew out the next day or the day after, I can't remember, and when he left, I had the strongest feeling, of adventure just over the horizon.

The day Jeremy left, I got my acceptance letter from the University of Colorado at Boulder. By late spring I was living in the Rockies, and could walk out my back door and climb into the Flatiron range. Months went by and I began to realize what getting a master's degree actually meant. I was studying medical anthropology, or how environmental and cultural factors affect disease. It was hugely demanding—you could read all day and still not keep up. I worried that maybe I wouldn't have time or energy to spare on a boyfriend who lived most of a continent away, and I sent Jer an emotionally cool letter reflecting my thinking.

I never heard back from him. By now he'd graduated college. I wasn't even sure where he was, which made me a little paranoid, not knowing what he was doing or thinking about me. I could have tracked him down if I'd really wanted to, but I'd worked myself into a state where I was too nervous to call him. As I got into my grad-school work, I stopped worrying about him. I had one particularly fascinating class examining mummies from ancient Nubia, in Africa, and by the end of the day, I'd have mummy dust all over my hands, which I figured was probably beneficial since they'd managed to survive for 3,000 years. Somewhere during my mummy period, I heard through the grapevine that Jeremy was living at home and working at a rental car company. Evidently he'd walked in to rent a car and come out a salesman. It soon became clear that he had a natural gift for figuring out how to talk to people. He was self-assured, personable. The buyer bought the product Jeremy was selling because he bought Jeremy.

One Saturday morning in May, Jimmy Best called. He had been skiing in the area and was in Boulder, which was a bit of a shock since it had been a year since I'd heard from Jeremy and longer still for Jimmy. The place we met for drinks limited you to two of their specially blended nuclear margaritas. It took me roughly one minute to ask about Jer and one margarita to gush over him. Jimmy and I went to a dance club and had far too many drinks and danced and laughed.

"He's dating someone," Jimmy said as we walked home.

"Me too," I said.

"It's not serious," he said.

"Me either," I said.

"I'll give you his number— Why don't you call him?" Jimmy said.

"Because I'm scared. But give him my number and tell him I love him."

The next evening when I returned from coaching gymnastics there was a message that Jer had called, and when I reached him it was like we hadn't missed a beat. There were no apologies, and no need for any. Jeremy had a new job, at a company in New York City that provided music stores with computerized kiosks containing information on thousands of artists and albums. Your daddy loved music, and here he was making real dollars selling a technology that hadn't existed five years earlier. He was living with his folks, but it wouldn't be long before he'd have enough money to get his own place.

He came out two weeks later to visit, and as soon as we got to my house from the airport, he disappeared into my bathroom for an unnaturally long time. He had a bad nosebleed, probably from the altitude—Boulder's up around 5,000 feet—and was freaking out that he'd messed up my sink.

"I do not care about the blood," I said through the door. "Now get out of my bathroom and sit with me."

I loved my life in Boulder and I showed it off to Jer, the dry brown magic of the mountains that makes you want to walk and bike and run and canoe and sit among them. We camped for several days on the outskirts of Rocky Mountain National Park. Jeremy—I dubbed him "pack mule"—hauled a trunk-size knapsack containing our gear and all sorts of savory food up the trail. We found a clearing near a stony cliff and pitched the tent. Nights were starry, cold, and clear. We talked about how separation, loneliness, misunderstandings, even anguish, had been for the best because we were young and those things had to be trotted out and detonated like little bombs. And anyway, most of life lay ahead. We talked about destiny and what it might mean when people keep returning to each other, despite their mistakes. We promised not to screw things up, not to desert each other again.

As we hiked back out, a violent spring thunderstorm broke, and we stumbled down the mountain trail under a barrage of lightning. By the time we hit the parking lot, we were wet and laughing. We stripped right there and changed into mismatched clothes we found in the car.

Saying good-bye to your father at the airport in Denver was one of the harder things I'd ever done. We soon developed a program in which every month, one of us visited the other one. In between, we ran up phone bills we could ill afford. Once I was temping at a fire station when I got a call from some cranky individual demanding that the fire department send a hook-and-ladder truck to rescue a cat up a tree. I was in the process of dragging out the directory to learn the protocol for a cat up a tree when I realized it was Jeremy. That sort of thing happened frequently.

We had little money, so when he came west we camped out at parks like Rocky Mountain National Park, northwest of Boulder, or Mesa Verde, in the southwest corner of Colorado, or Great Sand Dunes National Monument, halfway to the state's eastern border. Jeremy was the outdoorsman, hoisting our food cache far enough up a tree to keep bears away. He'd grow a little beard that came in with blond and red highlights and shave it off when he flew back east—Grizzly Adams for a week. I have pictures showing us wearing baseball caps sideways, making up foolish raps as we drove in my crumbling Bronco, or schussing down the immense Sahara-like dunes at the Great Sand Dunes. In another your father perches on a fence post with a herd of caribou behind him. We were like kids who'd been shut in for days and finally let out to play.

In the summer of 1995, a year after we started seeing each other again seriously, I completed the master's program and moved to Denver, hoping it would be easier to find a job there than in Boulder. But opportunities weren't as plentiful as I'd hoped. I was crying every time we said good-bye on the phone. One of us was going to have to move. While perusing the help wanted ads one morning in November it suddenly clicked that there really was no need to live in misery. Most of my friends and family were in the east and I was certain I could find a job in New York. I dialed Jeremy right away.

"What are you doing for Thanksgiving?" I said.

"Going, I guess, to Jennifer's with the family for—"

"Wrong. You're coming out here and taking me home," I said. "I can't do this anymore."

Jer dropped the phone and bellowed. He'd gotten what he'd been hoping for, more or less openly, since he was thirteen.

He flew out during Thanksgiving week and we skiied at Vail. He had enough money so we could stay in a decent hotel and have a nice dinner. Then we packed up a U-Haul and headed east. We had five delicious days doing everything we'd never been allowed to do on car trips—mostly wasting huge amounts of time in truck stops playing video games and eating cheeseburgers. By now Jeremy had moved into a decrepit loft on Warren Street in New York City, and when we arrived, he presented me with a care package of subway tokens and mace, the latter of which I really would have liked to use on the rat who ran around the loft. I quickly got a job at a small public relations firm and we moved into an apartment my parents owned at Eighty-fifth Street and Madison, a tiny studio. We were right on top of each other every minute we were together and it was fine.

While we were Christmas shopping on Fifth Avenue, I dragged him into Tiffany's.

"Let's look at rings," I said.

I pointed out a diamond on a six-pronged platinum setting, simple and traditional. From that day on, I kept tabs on Jeremy, because I figured he'd never be able to buy a ring without my knowing, especially as I'd call him at work to make sure he wasn't sneaking out. However, he started getting up before seven, which should have tipped me off since your daddy hated getting up early. He'd say he had to breakfast with some French clients, but of course—as I later learned—he was meeting with a jeweler. Nothing happened, though. January came and went, and with it my birthday. No ring. Then he took off for a quick trip with Jimmy Best. What I didn't know was that they'd gone up to Windham where Jeremy asked my father for permission to marry me.

"Why ask me?" Grandpa said. "It's your life."

Grandpa was secretly pleased that Jeremy had bothered to ask for his consent, especially when the answer was perfectly obvious, because Grandpa thought Jeremy was close to the ideal husband for me. But just to mess with him, he made him wait until the following morning to ask Grandma, so that Jer spent the whole night sweating bullets. Grandma, of course, was all for it.

A couple of days later, Jeremy took me to the Royalton Hotel. He told me that someone at work said there was

a really good martini bar there. Jer seemed excessively nervous, worried for some reason. The bar was crowded, and as
soon as we arrived he sucked down a martini. *What is wrong
with him?* I thought. *He's drinking too much too fast. I'm going
to be hanging out with* this *all night?*

"Let's sit over here," he said a bit stiffly, indicating the
white banquettes sprinkled around the lobby. He knelt, dug
into his jacket pocket, pulled out a royal blue ring box, and
asked me to marry him.

Being asked wasn't a bolt from heaven, but he'd made the
circumstances so mysterious that it actually took me by surprise, and brought me to tears. I said, "Yes, what took you so
long?"

He unfurled other surprises throughout the evening. Instead of the hamburger joint where we'd been planning to
have dinner, we ate in the hotel, where he'd gotten us a
room, though at the time we had little money. In the room
was my suitcase, packed with a choice of coordinated outfits
for work the next day, complete with matching belts and
shoes.

"I'm just waiting for the helicopter that lands on the roof
and takes us to our private island," I said.

"Should be along any minute," he said.

We were married on Labor Day weekend 1996, in an old
stone church in Windham in front of 250 guests. The wedding was nondenominational since Jeremy was Jewish and I
was raised in the Dutch Reformed faith. It was a hot day
and I had trouble getting what the minister was saying

because our hands were so sweaty that we were dripping on the floor and trying not to crack up about it. The reception brought all of our various circles of friends together for the first time, a raucous party stretching across several days.

"Okay, let's thank the Little Man," said Jeremy as we lay together in bed the night before we left on our honeymoon.

"Yeah. *Finally.* Maybe he needs to go to a special school or something. His techniques aren't up to date. He needs to go to magic chess school," I said.

"When he gets bored, that's when stuff happens," he said.

"That's when he came up with Dorrian's. 'Let's have Jeremy walk in the door at Dorrian's,' " I said.

"Then he's like, 'Let's get Jimmy Best involved here and send him out to Colorado,' " he said.

"Right. Then he wiped out all the jobs in Denver so I'd have to come back," I said.

We honeymooned in Bali, which is part of Indonesia, the world's most populous Muslim nation, a fact that had no significance for us at the time. For the first five days, we stayed in a thatched bungalow with no electricity in a fishing village on the northern coast. We'd be awakened by an army of roosters and head out for breakfast accompanied by a gang of children attracted to Jeremy because he was a foot taller than anyone else in town. There were nappy dogs and cats showing their ribs, but the people were well-fed and friendly. Hinduism is quite prevalent in Bali, and Jeremy was impressed by the offerings of palm leaf and incense in little red flowers left at the temples. Later we moved inland to Ubud. To get into town we had to walk through the monkey forest, and by the time we headed back to our hotel it was dark. The monkeys howled at us from above making a terrifying racket—fifteen minutes feeling our way home through a dark forest surrounded by invisible screaming monkeys. We were convinced we'd be discovered months later, bones picked clean, massacred by monkeys. We found the monkeys fascinating, and subsequently spent a lot of time in the forest, albeit in daylight. They'd leap onto me and reach into my pocket to get a candy bar I didn't even know I had.

Our next stop was the island of Sumbawa, a few hundred miles east of Bali. To get there we flew an antiquated and frightening turbo-prop plane operated by an Indonesian airline that specializes in island hopping. Going from Bali to Sumbawa, you leave the vivid greens of the rain-soaked jungle ecosystem and enter a drab, arid environment similar to Arizona. We drove south through Sumbawa and boarded a boat for the tiny island of Komodo, making our way across swirling, dangerous eddies. Several hours into the journey, the boat stopped.

"You swim here," said one of the crewmen.

When we got in, the water was warm and black and turbulent.

"Are there sharks?" Jeremy shouted at the boat.

"Yes," someone shouted back.

I looked over at Jer, bobbing next to me, and he was grinning. For some reason, he'd never looked better than at that moment, his tanned upper body above the water exposing the small tattoo on his left shoulder blade, a yin-yang symbol encircled by a ring of Saturn. I smiled back and we kept swimming, though nearer the boat.

We arrived at Komodo after dark. We slept onboard, tugging our mattress up to the roof where it was cooler. I pointed out the constellations of the southern hemisphere, which I'd learned in Australia. The next morning, we saw the Komodo dragons, enormous, ancient lizards that can kill and eat a full-size deer. Our guide poked at them through the fencing with a stick, which infuriated the little dinosaurs. They lashed their tails and snapped their jaws and ran about at alarming speed. I kept getting closer to them and Jeremy got upset, shouting at me to move away. The dragons lived in caves, which were spattered with blood.

The boat ride back took seven hours, and the water was so rough that we were seasick throughout—so sick, in fact, we couldn't climb down from the roof to the deck. Yet we were so high from being with each other that we laughed through it, even when they served us our third consecutive meal of fish heads and rice.

"*Fiiiish* heads," said Jeremy, shoving the plate toward my nose and smacking his lips.

"Stop it," I said.

Upon our return to Sumbawa, we had a bit more time on the island, which in contrast to Bali, is almost entirely Muslim and poor even by Indonesian standards, with many of the inhabitants eking out a living as salt farmers. Most of the women covered their faces. Nobody seemed to be smiling, and there were a great many people with physical deformities. We stayed at a crummy hotel near the airport, and we were so hot and dirty after the boat that we headed straight for the pool, even though it smelled bad and was patrolled by mangy dogs and a small, sex-crazed monkey who tried to straddle the dogs. As we approached, he charged with bared fangs. We dived into the pool and treaded water in the middle as the monkey leaped up and down and screamed.

"Why were you pushing me at the monkey?" I said.

"No, no, no, I was protecting you," Jer laughed, and splashed the monkey, who ran to the edge of the pool, howling and drooling. We debated whether monkeys can swim. After half an hour in the stagnant waters of our Sumbawan resort, we looked up and realized he'd gone.

We flew out the next day on the first leg of a long series of relays back to the States. From the air, Sumbawa was brown and yellow, its hills swathed in shadows by the clouds, a place that seemed trapped in a different pocket of time from our own. I thought of Bali and Kenya and Sumbawa, and how oblivious Americans are to how little the rest of the world resembles the United States. But the rest of the world was slowly disappearing through the window of the plane, and we were heading home to begin something of our own that had nothing to do with any of that. Or so I imagined as I leaned my head on Jeremy's shoulder, closed my eyes, and went to sleep.

Memory Box

Happy Easter! Emerson with bunnies, spring 2002.

Dear Emmy,

I flew for the first time since your daddy's death when I visited Shanksville in early March, shortly before the six-month anniversary of the attacks. The flight came courtesy of the *Today* show, which wanted to interview some of the Flight 93 women and film us walking around the site. Lisa Beamer and I made the trip along with Alice Hoglan, the mother of Mark Bingham, a former rugby player who was one of those who apparently charged the cabin.

"Are you okay to fly?" my mother asked.

"Sure, because I know what happens in a crash and it doesn't hurt. You just blow up. And I'll have Emmy with me and we'll simply, poof, disappear, and go right up there to Jeremy," I told her.

"That is such an awful thing to say," she said. "How can you talk like that?"

It was my life and my husband, so I was of the opinion that I had the right to give her the unvarnished truth as I saw it.

I thought making the trip under the auspices of a television program would at least get my butt back on an airplane.

I was fine as we boarded, but you were no sooner settled in my lap than you pointed at the telephone on the seat back in front of us and said excitedly, "Da da da da." I have no idea how you formed that association, but watching your face, it seemed genuine, and I had my usual reaction to such things, which was to cry and to try to hide from you the fact that I was crying.

I felt I owed it to myself to take a second look at the crash site, this time in a somewhat more composed frame of mind than I'd been in immediately after losing your daddy. And my curiosity had been awakened by our meeting with coroner Wally Miller in Woodbridge a few weeks earlier. Now Miller met us at the gate to the site in Shanksville and gave us a tour of the entire area. On a little hill overlooking where the plane went down there was a makeshift memorial containing things that visitors from all over the country had brought. Banners and flags and flowers. There was a line of wooden angels painted red, white, and blue, one for each of the passengers. The excavation and mapping of the "impact zone" were complete, and all was peaceful and empty. The little flags and mounds of earth and bulldozers were gone. The gangs of investigators and laborers and technicians were gone. There was no longer a hole in the ground to mark where the plane disappeared, but Miller took us to the spot where it had been, which was surrounded by a fence and still off-limits.

The weather was, once again, inhospitable. Spring was only weeks away, but a strong wind put an arctic bite into the air.

"So what did you find? Did you find organs? Did you

find skulls?" I heard myself ask through chattering teeth. So much for being timid about the details.

"We didn't find anything that size," Miller said. He explained that since the human body is mostly fluid, it explodes like a water balloon when subjected to the violent trauma of a plane crash, leaving bone and teeth but no intact soft tissue. Parts of hands and feet were recovered because they are strung together with tougher connective tissues. It was exactly as I'd explained to my mother: Such a crushing impact compresses the moment during which a human being can sustain a feeling of pain into an impossibly brief period of time. This realization was the mental novocaine that took the sting out of the horrific details I was learning. Life simply became death, as though there were no border between them.

We couldn't stay outside for very long due to the temperature, and we continued the discussion in Miller's car, with Lisa Beamer asking her questions, while I continued to be insatiable for detail. I asked if we could go to the hangar where all the personal effects found by the searchers had been marshaled.

"That's under FBI authority," Miller said. "We can't just walk in over there."

I didn't like that very much, but I also knew that Miller would do just about anything to help the families. He'd been fighting to have the land turned into a memorial. He'd given us all his cell-phone number and made himself available to answer questions around the clock. Wally Miller was the nearest thing to a hero the crash investigation had produced—and he was pretty near to one. Bringing the families together in Woodbridge had been his idea, not the government's. After the FBI had packed up and gone home, Miller arranged for firemen and emergency medical technicians from thirteen counties in western Pennsylvania to continue combing the site. He also brought down the National Guard, and then rounded up a bunch of guys he grew up with to go out and try yet another sweep. If Miller said I couldn't go over to the hangar, then I couldn't go.

Two types of personal effects had been found and cataloged. The associated items were those that came with some identifier marking them clearly as the property of a particular person. These were in the process of being returned to the families, and while unlikely to amount to much, Miller promised they would be in our possession within a few weeks. The unassociated effects had no personal identifiers. They'd be photographed and placed in a book so we could examine them and claim those that belonged to our loved ones.

For weeks, I had been thinking about Jeremy's wedding ring with the fervor of a zealot. The adverse portents for its recovery detected by Lauren the psychic only made me hunger for it more. I couldn't leave without learning its fate. Miller called over on his cell phone to the Douglass Personal Effects Administrators, a mortuary used by United Airlines that had the unassociated items, and I described it—an etched platinum band big enough to fit Jeremy's outsized finger. It wasn't there. That wasn't a revelation, since this was probably the sixth time I'd had someone call about the ring, or called myself, but I'd hoped somehow Miller would get a different result. That ring had become a talisman of Jeremy to me.

"So what am I getting back?" I asked Miller when he got off the phone.

"A credit card," he said. "It got melted some but it's mostly intact."

"That's it?" I said. "What about the other families?"

"You're getting a good bit less than some of the other families, that's the way it looks to me," he said.

"Maybe something else will turn up," I said.

"Not likely," he said. "The search is over."

My chin quivered. Lisa Beamer was sitting next to me. She looked at me in a certain way that said, *Girl, you had better see the black humor in this or you really are lost.*

My chin stopped quivering.

"If you don't find that ring, I'm coming down with my metal detector this summer," I said.

"Hey, I'll help you look," he laughed.

"Deal," I said.

"I wouldn't be surprised if you don't both wind up down here digging around like two crazy lunatics," said Lisa.

Of course, I was soon back in New Jersey, alone, without the steadying influence of Lisa. I couldn't help thinking about that damned ring—like, if I thought about it enough, that would somehow capture it for me, force it to come back to me. Every night, before I went to bed, I'd say to myself, *You know you're going to find it,* like a prayer. I speculated with Kim and Jim about whether platinum melts easily, and then I went out and asked some jewelers. I designed myself a new ring, incorporating pieces from both Jeremy's (once found) and mine, along with something else symbolizing you, Emmy. I never did decide what.

Around this time, my therapy group was supposed to be reading a book called *When Bad Things Happen to Good People*. None of us really read it, but I glanced through it and was struck by a section that said, don't pray for things that have already happened because you can't affect them. That seems obvious, I know, but it sufficed to knock the legs out from under my ring delusion. That trite passage was the only thing I retained from the book but it did the job.

I told my therapy group about my newfound perspective on the ring.

"I liked it better when I was still hoping I'd get it back," I said. "Now it feels like I'm looking ahead and there's nothing."

A few days later, I was traveling again, making my third visit to the White House, the story of which easily shrinks into a few sentences. The president spoke, this time to a large group, perhaps a thousand people—9/11 families who had assembled in the Rose Garden for the six-month anniversary of the attacks. The president's speech seemed like any other speech, it didn't survive long in my memory. By the time I got back to the hotel, you were feverish and vomiting, and I vividly remember being in a strange room in a strange building in a strange city and realizing that I alone was responsible for you. What frightened me wasn't the sleep I'd miss because no one else would go to you when you cried out during the night. It was that I had been deprived forever of the comfort of knowing there was *someone else*.

My brother Pieter called my room from his room. He

was going out with his girlfriend for drinks and did I want to come?

I can't, I said. Emmy's sick.

Then there was the relief of returning to the Greenwood Lake house, with the sand that spattered across the road from the lake and the smell of woods by the water. Back here at the house, I had more of a sense of control, though I knew I had to keep working on it, like conditioning an atrophied muscle. So I was glad I was parked in front of our A&P when I opened the package containing Jeremy's credit card. Because the whole point was not to fall apart at home, in front of you.

Our funeral home in Windham had forwarded the credit card from the authorities at Shanksville, who also sent the funeral home Jeremy's remains, which I assumed were teeth. The credit card came in a package with a catalog of coffins I'd requested from the funeral home—page after page of caskets, ideas on how to entomb your loved one.

Jer: What would Dracula pick?
Me: A nice black one.

That was the conversation playing in my head while I was looking at the catalog. Then I thought about how the real Jeremy, the one who used to live with me, not the one who makes up lines for himself in my head, how the real Jeremy once told me he didn't want to be buried in the ground. Well, I thought, you're really not. All that's going into this box are some teeth. The rest of you is pretty much everywhere, if you think about it.

Next to the coffin catalog was a formal white envelope of the kind used for invitations. It contained an embossed piece of paper reading: "Associated property for Jeremy Glick. The enclosed items should be considered sensitive material due to conditions." The credit card had been scorched and the left corner was missing, but you could see the American Airlines insignia—it was a frequent flier credit card—and some other corporate logos. Someone had carefully taped the card back together along one edge. The raised numbers down the center had collapsed in the intense heat. The silvery parts of the card were brown with dirt. Jer's signature had disappeared from the back.

I realized it almost had to be the card he used to phone me that morning, sliding it through the slot in the Airphone on the seat back in front of him. *It's just a credit card, get a grip,* I thought.

I called Jimmy Best. He could hear I was in a state.

"Why'd you open it in the parking lot?" he wanted to know.

"I had to just open it," I said. "I didn't ponder over it. It happened."

Some time later, I visited another psychic, this time in the nearby town of Kinnelon. Lauren had charged me $150, which seemed like an awful lot, but this woman, completely for free, told me I would receive something from the crash bound in leather. I have to say, I took her with a grain of salt, but it was a much smaller grain than it would have been before I saw Lauren. I thought *a lot* about what I might be getting back. Instead of saying my ring prayer, now I wondered what this retrieved object might be. What could possibly have survived that blast furnace that turned steel and platinum into dust and vapor?

Of course, I knew the black-box recorder had survived to bear witness to what happened in the front of the airplane, and maybe ten days after I returned from the White House, I got a call from the FBI, a female agent. They'd decided to let us hear the tape. We were to be summoned to "a location" where all of us would sit in a room and listen together. We could hear it as many times as we wanted that day. I'd hoped to play it in my home, where I could spend time with it alone, stopping and starting as I pleased. Few things could be more private than my husband's last moments. I didn't want anyone around me.

"I'm sorry," said the FBI woman. "For security reasons, it's got to be handled this way."

Lots of people thought I shouldn't drive down alone to hear the tape. Kim was afraid something would happen if I chauffeured myself. My dad wanted to fly up, rent a car, make a day of it. Jennifer and Oma Glick were going to hear the black box tape also, but in their own car, which was the way I wanted it. I stuck to my guns. I drove myself.

"If I get to where I'm not okay to drive, I'll pull over," I said.

The Princeton Hyatt, where the black box was to be played, is in central New Jersey. The hotel was secure inside but chaos outside. Lisa Beamer and I arrived at about the same time, dashing from the parking lot into the lobby past a mass of barking reporters. Inside were dozens of police, who searched us and checked our identification. The FBI wanted Flight 93 families to provide them with "victim impact statements," verbal accounts of how the death of your loved one affected the survivors. Prior to playing the black box, they planned to take our statements for use in the Moussaoui trial and perhaps in the trials of other suspected terrorists as well. But Lisa and I were among the few who had decided not to do it. I didn't think I was capable of sitting in a hotel room and making someone understand what Jeremy was to me. To enumerate all the things that were now absent simply didn't seem possible. So Lisa, Oma, Jennifer, and I snuck out for coffee. We found a quiet place in Princeton.

"You know, here we're having this very normal moment, but in ten minutes, we're going to hear the sickest, most screwed-up thing," I said. "Now how do you balance that?"

Lisa didn't know and neither did I.

When we got back to the Hyatt, they seated us in uncomfortable blue chairs in a banquet room on the first floor. Lisa and I sat near the back so we could leave quickly if we felt the need. There was a long table in the front of the room on which you were supposed to put your purse or whatever you were carrying. They covered it all with a sheet so you couldn't have access to your stuff while they played the tape. Someone from the National Transportation Safety Board, the federal agency charged with investigating plane crashes, gave us a primer on how a black box works. It's actually painted orange for visibility and located in the back of the aircraft. It records in thirty-minute loops, a record of the last half-hour of the airplane's life. Its microphone system picks up sound very well in the cockpit and more faintly back to perhaps the first row of first class. The relative loudness of things—and what that might mean—is a critical issue, as we were about to learn.

We put on huge headphones. I had to hold my hands over my ears to keep them on. The lights were dimmed and they started the tape. There was a large screen in front of us on which was projected a running transcript of every word, cough, or cry. Along one side of the transcript was a digital tally that ticked off the minutes and seconds. The transcript ran a little ahead of the tape for better comprehension. When the hijackers spoke Arabic, as they frequently did, it was simultaneously translated into English on the screen.

I was getting used to all of this when I heard the faint voice of a woman pleading for her life, probably the stewardess in first class whom the FBI believed had been mortally wounded when the terrorists broke into the flight deck. For quite a while after that, very little happened. There was muttering, papers being shuffled. The hijackers were apparently confused by certain equipment in the cockpit. It's not until near the end of the tape that you become vaguely aware that something is starting to happen. The tempo is building. There's some agitated discussion among the terrorists. You hear thumping. And then the attack, or whatever it is, begins. Glass is shattering. There is shouting and screaming. And I remember thinking, *Unbelievably loud! They're in the cockpit!* I heard your daddy's grunt, his judo grunt, his sound, a trademark. I heard it, amid sharp banging sounds and a fury of cries, I knew right away that I was hearing him fighting. I was hearing it amidst all that lethal chaos.

Then you heard someone yell, "Pull up! Get her up!"

And then the wind. For quite a while, a rushing of wind.

I knew silence was what was coming next. I didn't want to stick around for that silence because it frightened me more than anything I'd heard, and I was afraid I'd never get that silence out of my head. I ran from the banquet room and crumpled into a chair in the hallway. One of the people whose job it was to come up to you and ask if you were all right approached and started to say something.

"Get away from me," I said.

I accepted a cup of water from someone. I was freezing cold, shaking, sick. People started to come out through the banquet room doors and I got up numbly and went back in to get my purse. An official approached me.

"Do you want to hear it again?" he asked very gently.

I shook my head.

I found Lisa and Oma and said good-bye. I was about to beeline for the front door when I was intercepted by an FBI agent.

"Let me walk you," he said. "It's pretty crazy out there."

With four huge FBI men forming a kind of human quadrangle around me, we busted our way through the media pack just beyond the front door, and it was well that I had bodyguards, because I was in a daze and there were a hundred reporters who'd been kept outside all day, away from the story, who desperately wanted somebody to say something to them. And it seemed to me that whoever was the first to be dangled before those reporters would become a human sacrifice, just stripped to the bone with questions. So I was grateful to reach my car unmolested. I got in and sat for a moment. I wondered what happened to Lisa. Then

I remembered that she had very cleverly parked in a service lot around back, and probably just strolled to her car, driving away unnoticed.

I took a breath, started the car. I turned on the radio, and on came a song that Jer and I loved so much. It was our wedding song. Al Green.

Baby let's, let's stay together

I took another breath and drove away.

When I got home I called Lisa.

"Made a clean getaway, huh?" I said.

"Not really," she said.

Turned out she'd succeeded in driving away without being spotted, got one block and realized she'd forgotten her cell phone. Reporters swarmed her like wet bees the moment she got back to the hotel. It's Lisa Beamer! *She must have come back to make some kind of statement!*

"I have nothing to say," she shouted as she leapt out of her car. "I forgot my stupid phone."

We got a good laugh out of it.

You didn't make the trip to the Hyatt for the black box. I left you behind with Ute, the nanny who'd just started taking care of you. Ute was German, spoke English as well as I did, and by entering my life at this time had walked into a strangely American maelstrom. She was willowy, chocolate-haired with porcelain skin, twenty-six but worldly. She was mature, and she had to be to handle a woman she scarcely knew returning home after hearing the tape of her husband's death. Not that I was hysterical or launched into a monologue. I couldn't dissect what I'd heard. It was lodged whole in my imagination, like something I'd almost choked on.

Ute listened as I talked fuzzily at her.

"It's terrible because you listen, but you don't really know what's happening. You can guess, but . . . you don't *want* to guess," I said.

I told her I'd heard they were thinking of releasing the transcript of the black box to the public, which I thought would be a terrible mistake. I explained how some months earlier, ABC News called to tell me that the air traffic control tape, which captured the sound of the terrorists overpowering the flight crew, was being released. All I could think of was Sandy Dahl, the wife of the captain, and Melody Homer, who was married to the copilot and has a daughter your age. And now the whole world is hearing your husband be murdered.

Ute nodded.

"I was just glad you were here with my daughter," I said.

She smiled.

"I love being with her," she said.

It was remarkable how quickly I got used to having another pair of hands, but that didn't mean I wasn't overjoyed to have them. Having Ute move in was almost like gaining a cheery, scrubbed younger sister, who was quick to pick up my spirits, but kept out of the way when there was nothing useful to say. She was energetic at making up games or running you up to the park so you would be with other children. She got me to go out more just to be with the two of you. There was no question she loved you like a baby sister.

Ute pitched in with chores around the house, but one place that was never scrubbed or dusted was the area of my desk where I planned to keep the things of Jeremy's found in Shanksville. So far, the credit card, still in its white envelope, was all there was to my collection, though I had hopes for more. Not that I was done with the card, which wound up being used once more, as it turned out. I was by now used to receiving promotional offers and bills and frequent flier statements and other things addressed to Jeremy L. Glick. And gradually, over time, I halted the flow of official business to your dad. Frequently, telling the affected company that my husband died during the 9/11 attacks settled the matter quickly and simply.

Because I had gone ahead and canceled Jer's credit card, the E-Z Pass people—the ones who administer the automatic highway toll system in New Jersey and neighboring states—sent me a letter that his card was no good, and I had to arrange for a different way to pay for my E-Z Pass. I called them, but when I tried to give them a new credit card after an hour and a half on hold, they said they needed my password, which only Jeremy knew. It didn't matter that he had died on 9/11—without the password, I would need to complete some forms.

"Couldn't we skip that?" I said, a little impatiently.

"Yes, if you've got your old credit card," they said.

"Actually, I do," I said, reaching for it. "The plane crash investigators just returned it to me."

I started to read the numbers, but I couldn't make out the last one.

"I can't tell if it's a six or a nine because it's very badly damaged," I said, starting to lose my composure. I was still kind of raw about this credit card. Looking at it affected me powerfully.

"We need the full sequence of numbers," said E-Z Pass. "It's okay. We'll send you the form. Just takes a second to fill it out."

The E-Z Pass people proved implacable, and indeed, now it seems almost funny. Maybe I can get Jeremy to phone from heaven to tell them whether it was a six or a nine. I just hope he can remember his password, or he could be in real trouble.

Ana San Juan, who'd been my roommate in Boulder, flew in from Colorado to drive with me, Ute, and you to Windham for the burial. The "remains" had by now been placed in the coffin I'd ordered from the coffin catalog that arrived with the credit card. Also in the coffin was a "memory box" containing things people wanted buried with Jeremy. In the end, I realized the memory box was one of those details that Jeremy almost certainly would have dispensed with if he'd been making his own funeral arrangements. It was way too much work. I pecked away all week on the letter that I put in the box, but it wasn't like talking to him in a dream where I'd feel a kind of glow all the next morning. I wrote it only because I felt the weight of the dead on me to furnish something to go into the ground with him. Then I had to make sure all our dozens of friends and relatives got their memory box stuff in on time, because there was a deadline for the memory box to go into the coffin.

Jer: A coffin deadline? You're kidding.
Me: 'Fraid not, Dracula.

I knew I was luckier than some of the women in my therapy group. Our group talked a lot about funerals—we had the experience of sudden death in common, after all. And periodically, someone in the group would want to discuss how a cop had showed up at her door to tell her that some sliver of her husband had been found. There was a steady trickle of these kinds of stories in group, a continual process that went on for maybe a year, because there were thousands of pieces of people out there to be found. Some women learned in the first couple of weeks that a body part or some object had been located. Some women never got anything.

One woman's son died at the World Trade Center. No trace of him was ever found, not so much as a scrap of paper from his pocket. She started to tell us in group about a friend of hers who had just lost a son in a motorcycle accident. He was such a young man and it was terrible, but at least there was a body and a grave, somewhere to go to grieve. Because you're supposed to have a place to go. So people in group started suggesting that maybe she could bury a memory box, and put things in it that were his. And then she'd have a place to go.

As we drove up to Windham for the burial. I told Ana I felt a *little* lucky to have something to bury, not just that memory box. We got off the New York State Thruway and drove through the Catskills on Route 23 in my Jeep, then into the little town of Windham. A few miles farther along, I looked out the window to my right, and there was Pleasant Valley Cemetery, which runs up a fairly steep slope of hill. And near the top of the hill, in the brilliant relief of the morning sun, were two men digging my husband's grave. I looked at Ana, next to me, and she looked back at me, thinking, *We're here to bury him*. We panicked. I started to cry.

After a mile or so Ana found her voice.

"So what we're going to do is, we're going to come up with a game plan," she said.

"Make it good, because this is not going the way I'd hoped," I said.

Ana's plan was to keep moving, attend to the details of the funeral, stay immersed in the physical world—always a good strategy. We went back to the house, fed you lunch, called some people. Then I left you in the care of Ute for your nap and escaped with Ana to the church where Jer and I were married, and where I'd gone to speak to him the first time, the day after he died. It's an early nineteenth-century stone church on a small hill looking out over the mountains, with a little arboretum on the side. I asked Ana to wait outside, and I entered the church, which had been closed for the winter. Inside, I was alone, and it was cold and dark. My mind emptied and I inhaled the cold air and looked into the blackness.

We went down to the funeral home from the church so

I could spend some time with the coffin, which was sitting in its place, surrounded by flowers, a huge, lustrous piece of cherry-red oak. We cried some more, and then I started wondering, what's in there? Because somehow, despite my curiosity about so many things, and though I knew about the teeth being discovered, I'd never found out what the funeral home was actually planning to bury in that coffin. And just at that moment, I couldn't really puzzle out why I hadn't.

We sat quietly for about an hour, and then I said, "Ana, if I asked them to open it, would they open it?"

"God, I don't know. They'd have to, wouldn't they?" she said.

"Yeah. I mean, it's Jer. He's mine. I could run out of here with it and do whatever I want," I said.

We had quite a debate about this. Do you want to open it? Do you not want to open it? Do you want me to get the funeral director? Do you think he's around? Well, if he isn't, we could get him. Okay, so should I get him?

In the end, we didn't get him.

It's all very well to have a spiritual connection with someone you love, but sometimes, I have an overwhelming desire to be with your daddy physically. There was even a part of my mind that didn't accept that he was gone, because he died so far away, in a remote field, and I didn't see it happen. I wanted him as close to me as I could have him, and for a minute, seeing what was in the coffin seemed like it might help. In the next breath, I realized there was no way to get back to the physical, and all I would be doing was making certain that whatever *was* in the coffin would be

laser-engraved on my brain. That seemed a risky proposi-
tion at best.

Then Ana said, "You know, Lyz, maybe we're just being
too serious here. Jeremy would laugh about this. Don't you
think? I mean, let's just say it's a couple of teeth in there. Jeremy would be like, 'You guys are what? Sitting around in a
little room paying respects to my teeth? You've got to be
kidding.' He'd have us cracking up about this."

We spun out a scenario about how Jeremy was standing
by the coffin, pointing at it and then pointing at us, and going, *You're doing what now? You're praying to my molars?* in his
voice. And I had to laugh, the little hiccup laugh you have
when you laugh right after you've been crying, a laugh of
infinite relief. Ana and I sat a while longer. We started to
feel hungry, and we got in the Jeep and went back up to the
house and had pizza. I was glad Ana was sleeping in the
house with you and me that night.

The burial was on Friday, May 17, eight months and six
days after the crash, a delay caused by the time it took to
process all the remains found at the crash site. It was raining
and we were gathered a bit awkwardly under a tent pitched
sideways on a hill. There were fifty of us around the grave,
Grandpa and Grandma and all the Glicks, except Jeremy's
brother Jonah, who had just gotten married and was living
in Japan. All the close friends were there, like Jimmy and
Kim and Ronnie Zaykowski and Ana and Shari and Diana.
You were at home with Ute.

I read a poem by Henry Scott Holland, the one that begins, "Death is nothing at all/I have only slipped away into the next room." I had trouble getting through it, but the lines, "Wear no forced air of solemnity or sorrow/Laugh as we always laughed at the little jokes we enjoyed together," precisely express the way I think of your daddy.

Then the minister who married us, Reverend Steven Yon, spoke.

"Fertile ground for the germination of hatred, desire for vengeance, bitterness and despair has been cultivated," he said "If we're not careful, our hearts can be made dark by this great harm that has been done."

He said he didn't really believe in this idea that we can have closure on our personal tragedies and doubted we'd ever find anything like that with Jeremy. That struck a chord with me. *I don't want closure. I want continuance.* After the eulogy, in accordance with Jewish tradition, everyone pitched a shovelful of earth onto the coffin, which I found terribly sad, but then the sun came out and pierced the tent, warming the back of my neck, like when it shone down on your crib the morning after the crash.

Most of our friends started walking down the hill from the grave. We all headed right across Route 23 to the Brandywine. The Brandywine is a restaurant and bar whose windows look out over the cemetery and the mountain behind it. You made an appearance with Ute during lunch in your light pink Easter dress with the bow in the back, and I took you home for your nap. After changing into jeans, I returned to the grave, now covered with fresh soil. I lay down on it and rolled back and forth in the sun and cried, just finally let everything out, which felt so good that I lay out there on my back for half an hour.

One of your daddy's friends from Alpha Delta Phi, John Sinacori, was sitting at the bar at the Brandywine staring out at the cemetery. He was draining his fifth beer when he saw something fluttering around the freshly dug grave.

"What the hell is that?" he said.

He turned to his wife. "I just saw something fly out of Jeremy's grave. I'm not kidding."

Eyes rolled up into heads at this, but John was sure he'd seen Jeremy's ghost. I burst in, covered with hay and dirt.

"Where you been, Lyzzy?" someone asked.

"Didn't you see me? I was rolling on Jeremy's grave," I said. "And hey, that's *before* I had a drink."

Everyone laughed except John, who missed your daddy as much as anyone and had been perfectly happy to believe he'd seen his ghost. We went to another bar and stayed into the evening, in fact, until the bar closed, and most of us got as drunk as humanly possible. I'd planned to spend the next morning at the grave, but eight inches of snow fell, though it was the middle of May, which I took as a hint that my presence wasn't required. By the following afternoon the snow had mostly melted, and I drove back to Hewitt knowing I'd buried everything there was to bury.

Perhaps it was having Ute in the house, but I found myself going out a bit more frequently that spring. I saw friends a little more often. I went into New York to see Shari. I didn't really feel better, but I couldn't sit around the house. There were still phone calls from reporters to dodge, and memorials to attend. The mayor of Hewitt led a group of hikers up a winding mountain trail that your daddy and I used to hike frequently, now renamed the Jeremy Glick Trail. The trail leads to a little body of water called Surprise Lake, and there's an extensive view from the top of the mountain. Thirty people made the trip with us on a very hot day, and when we got to the top, the mayor read a proclamation. I dug my nails into my palm, but I cried anyway behind my sunglasses, and you cried a little too from your perch on Ute's back. Hawks glided in the updrafts above the summit as we walked back down.

I parked the Jeep in the garage at the house and extricated you from your car seat. Hung upon the garage wall was Jer's wake board, a kind of extrawide water ski similar in design to a snowboard, and I realized it was turning summer, but Jer wouldn't be putting his boat in the water. I looked around the garage at his wet suit, his mountain bike, his weights, his golf clubs. All the things that we did together at the beginning of each season, I would do alone. I carried you inside and fixed you something to eat. If I go one day past the present, I panic, but caring for you gives me a routine here in the present. I changed out of my hiking clothes, went to the closet to get my shoes and found a manila folder sitting on top of them. *How did this get here?* I hadn't seen it when I'd rummaged in there before.

In it was a postcard I'd written to Jer when I was in Colorado. There was also the bill for his college loans—

$28,000!—and next to that was a partly filled-out application to attend the United States Olympic Team's training camp in Colorado Springs. I vaguely remembered him mentioning the idea of joining the Olympic judo team, but I'd had no idea he'd actually begun the application process. I called Jimmy Best at work.

"Oh yeah, he had big plans about going to Colorado and training, and that way he could be with you," said Jimmy. "You were still out there and you guys weren't an item yet."

"He was going to move to Colorado Springs? You're kidding," I said.

"No, I'm not kidding. After he won the collegiate title, the U.S. judo team invited him to train with them. He'd been doing this all his life, and he wanted to take it to the next level. He could have done it. There were judo guys he knew on the team. Guys he'd beaten," said Jimmy.

"So why didn't he join?"

"He got that rental car agency job, the salesman job, which fell into his lap. And he was just such a natural at it. I mean, he could sell you your own shirt," he said.

"Plus twenty-eight thousand dollars in loans," I said.

"Had to take care of that," Jimmy said. "You came east. End of story."

I thought about what might have happened if he hadn't taken that first job, and instead had tried out for the Olympic team. I wondered how tough it would have been on him physically. He had been injured so many times in judo and wrestling over the years. Instead he went into sales, and wound up flying out to California on a particular morning in September and using what he knew in the cockpit of a plane.

This wouldn't have been Olympic-style judo, but its harsher side—judo the self-defense system, which is descended from the ancient Chinese art of jiu-jitsu and includes all the known methods for bare-handed killing, most of which are too dangerous for sporting judo. These are the choke holds and pressure points, the breaking of elbows, eye-gouging attacks, and other brutal disabling and killing techniques taught to police officers and the military. Sensei Ogasawara had instructed Jer in both sides of judo. He also taught that we have the right to survive violence, but no right to initiate it.

I forced my mind away from such uncomfortable thoughts. Instead I would remember that Jeremy, once again, had found a novel way to be close to me.

I went to bed thinking about Boulder, our camping trips, the mountains. That night, I had a vivid dream. I'm driving in my old Volkswagen bug. Next to me is an American Indian, who doesn't have the use of his legs. Yet he is doing the driving.

"Who are you?" I ask him.

He doesn't answer. I think a minute and say, "I know who you are."

"Of course you know me," he says. "We've always known each other."

I accept that. I look up in the sky and see huge eagle-like birds, dozens of them.

"My God, they're so beautiful, I can't believe I never noticed them before," I say.

"No, they're always there. You just need to open your eyes and look at them," he says. We sit in the car and watch the birds.

A few days later, I saw Helen, my longtime therapist, and told her about the dream.

"I've had such a peaceful feeling from that dream all week. A beauty like I cannot even describe," I said.

"You're an anthropologist," said Helen. "What do you know about big eagle-like birds in Native American culture?" Helen said.

"Absolutely nothing," I said.

"Go look it up," she said.

I located information on Indian folklore on the Internet and found a picture of a thunderbird. It was exactly the bird I'd seen in my dream, I just hadn't known the name for it. A mythical creature that is much bigger than an eagle, the thunderbird symbolizes the link between heaven and earth. Indeed, every culture, modern and ancient, seems to have a bird with the magical ability to slip the barrier between the two worlds, flying effortlessly back and forth. They are messengers from the gods and sometimes powerful warriors who wield the thunderbolt. Ancient Mesopotamia had a thunderbird called Imdugud. European cultures had the griffin and the phoenix, and in some parts of Asia, the bird was called garuda.

Now why in God's name would I have that dream? I thought. The nice part was, it comforted me even before I knew what it meant. Of course, now I believed the Indian was right. The birds *are* always there. It is, however, necessary to look up to see them.

Arrivals and Departures

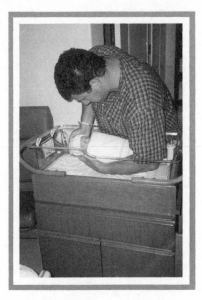

Here at last! Jeremy and Emmy,
Mt. Sinai Hospital, New York,
June 18, 2001.

Dear Emmy,

We walked into our place at Eighty-fifth and Madison and realized that we were home from Sumbawa and the sexually deranged monkey and everything else. We'd flown all the way back from the other side of the world for the privilege of sharing a space of perhaps 650 square feet. There was room for a bed, a fold-out sofa, and a couple of small tables, which happens to be exactly what we had in there. It may have been in a rather pricey neighborhood in Manhattan, but that didn't change the fact that the only alternative to hanging out in the main living area of our apartment was hanging out in the bathroom.

We'd discussed this with Reverend Yon during our mandatory premarital counseling session.

"What do you do when you get angry?" he asked us.

"Nothing," I said.

"Nothing," Jer said.

"Well, when was the last time you had a fight?"

"You mean, the last time I actually punched out her lights?" Jeremy said.

Reverend Yon looked like someone had bounced an iron block off his head.

"Kidding," said Jeremy. "I was joking."

"Oh." A nervous laugh from the good Reverend.

"You know, all married couples fight. About small things, big things. Where do you go when you need to slam a door and get away?" the Reverend said.

"We can't slam a door. It's a one-room apartment," I said.

"Okay, well, do you get in the car? Take a little drive?"

"We don't have a car," Jer said.

All of which was true. And frequently it wasn't just us in this tiny space, but friends like Shari or Ana sleeping on the pull-out couch that was eighteen inches from the edge of our bed, so it was like we were all in the same bed. Despite the cramped quarters, your dad and I got on well together right from the start, and it was surprising how quickly we started to feel like a couple of old shoes who'd been cohabitating forever. We didn't really fight, just some occasional glowering. The glowering side of Jeremy I called Heinrich. He called my glowerer Mona. This went back to high school when we invented Heinrich and Mona as a dysfunctional couple. Heinrich, the overbearing Type-A father figure, and Mona, his equally unpleasant man-eating companion. The Heinrich personality appeared frequently in traffic, like when we borrowed a car from Oma and Opa to go camping in the Adirondacks, as we often did in the summer. Jer would get stressed at jerks cutting him off and driving like neanderthals and he'd give them the finger.

"Okay, Heinrich, chill out," I'd say.

Once my dad was driving with us when it happened.

"Make you feel better to do that?" my dad asked him.

"Actually it does," Jeremy-Heinrich said.

For me, the Mona personality took over sometimes when I was packing or planning, and I'd begin to talk quickly and distractedly, as if not fully formed sentences were being spit out of my head due to some temporary electrical malfunction.

"Easy, there, Mona," Jeremy would say calmly, as though Jeremy-Heinrich had never existed.

Once you're married, you realize you are now committed to living with a whole person. You could never have observed all the other person's facets in the bits of time high school lovers spend together. Over the course of a marriage, some spouses are dealt a series of rude surprises about the person they married: *Have you met my swearing, snoring, toenail-clipper-losing, inept carpentering, philandering, occasionally drunk husband?* I never felt ambushed by my husband's bad qualities. We had every opportunity to make each other miserable in our tiny Manhattan den, but instead we felt the euphoria of high school lovers all over again. Of course, Jer and I only had five years of marriage, but the four spent in that micro-apartment were among our happiest times, and appearances by Jeremy-Heinrich and Lyz-Mona were rare.

We were out of doors a lot. Central Park was two blocks away. We'd run around the reservoir there together, two steps of mine for each of his. I'd wanted a pug all my life, so I took him to Pug Hill, which is a little area of the park near the statue of Alice in Wonderland where all the pugs go. And he fell in love with pugs, as I knew he would.

"It's a big dog in a little body," he said.

We bought Maxine and took her to Pug Hill. Jer got into the habit of carrying pocketfuls of biscuits for Maxine to eat during her walk. It didn't embarrass him when I dressed her up as a cowgirl for Halloween. "Put her hat on, she's looking good," he said. We'd trot her down toward the Metropolitan Museum of Art, or sometimes we'd have drinks on their rooftop deck. Other than that, we weren't much for the bar scene. We weren't much for cooking either. Jeremy liked Chinese food and steaks. I liked spaghetti. All were available in inexpensive restaurants, and with both of us working, we ate out virtually every night. We'd rent a movie and snuggle on the couch. We might have lived that way a good while longer but for wanting a baby.

During the several years following our marriage, your father moved restlessly through a series of jobs. He left Muze, the company that sold computerized kiosks to music stores, and joined E-Works, selling software. Five months later, he quit E-Works to sell hardware at Magna, where he was laid off after four months. He soon landed a job at double the salary at Giga, a much bigger Cambridge-based company that consults on computer technology issues. Even more important than Giga's size, they let him work from home.

However, Jeremy was worried he'd be seen as flitting from place to place.

"Great résumé," he said ruefully to my dad. "Three weeks here, two weeks there—"

"First of all, you're still young, and secondly, you're

moving for the right reasons," Grandpa said. "So don't worry about it."

I think Jer suspected Grandpa was right, but he wanted to hear it from someone he respected. He sought better money, but wanted other things more. He'd get frustrated with the lumbering pace of a company's decision-making, or get bored and want a bigger challenge. He also wanted time to ski and wake board, to indulge the rough-edged physicality that was so much a part of his life. Above all, he wanted time with me.

I found out later that back in college, he and Ron Zaykowski had talked about good ways and bad ways of achieving success.

"If you want to succeed, you can't do the things you enjoy or be with the important people in your life—I mean, what a crock," he said once. "People think it has to be that way. Bullshit."

Jer knew what he wanted, and it wasn't a job living on airplanes and sleeping in hotel rooms, putting on flab, answering to some petty dictator on the other end of a phone. Your daddy couldn't tolerate being under someone's thumb. For him it was call your own shot or find another game.

And he was confident he'd get what he wanted. There was evidence he was right. He was offered every job for which he interviewed. Indeed, he was doing fabulously well in his career. It was his body that began to betray him. He took a bad fall skiing and twisted his neck, triggering months of wasting pain. His accident would, in fact, have been relatively minor had he not already suffered so many serious blows to his head and neck over many years in wrestling and judo. The muscles in his left shoulder, chest, and arm atrophied, and the shoulder went numb. One day he was standing in front of the mirror and I came up behind him and we were both shocked. The pectoral muscles on the left had shrunk to half the size of those on the right. Unable to sleep, he'd squirm through the night. But Jer wouldn't go to a doctor until I gave him an ultimatum.

"Either go see somebody or stop expecting me to be sympathetic," I told him.

The diagnosis was a disc in the neck that was herniated so badly, it had to come out. So after a few weeks of poking and prodding and finally an operation during which a hole was cut in his neck and the disc scooped out, the doctors succeeded in putting Jer back into working order. And though some aches and pains remained, they no longer tortured him. Next it would be my turn with the doctors.

By now, I'd left the small public relations firm at which I'd been working ever since I'd moved into New York and started teaching social sciences at a business college in Manhattan. From the first, I'd seen the public relations job as temporary, while teaching had always fascinated me. Since my degree in anthropology was a master's, not a doctorate, I didn't have a great many options for college-level jobs, and once I made up my mind to start teaching, I simply took the first job I could get.

The business college where I teach is not Harvard. For

many of my students, English is, if not a second language, still not quite their first. Many wouldn't be able to go to college were it not for the internships at brokerages, banks, and law firms that help pay their way through school. I was assigned four social science classes per semester in subjects like geography and world cultures. My first day, the students were a bit shocked at how young I looked. But I wasn't intimidated by the murmuring and muttering. Nor was I put off by their sometimes childish attitudes toward the work, the silly excuses. And some were far from silly: *I couldn't do my homework because I'm a single mom and I don't have a babysitter. And my boyfriend is trying to steal the baby.* The classes I teach are working-class New York City, made up of anyone and everyone you might see in any of its neighborhoods—Italian kids from Howard Beach, Chinese and Ukrainians from the Lower East Side, Colombians from Washington Heights, and Nigerians and African-Americans from Flatbush.

"My race and ethnicity class at Colby was all white," I told Jer one day after class. "Now I'm teaching race and ethnicity and the class looks like the United Nations."

Despite my income as a teacher and Jer's success as a salesman, we never had much money, and what we did have ran through our fingers living in Manhattan—not that we minded spending it on camping trips or skiing or whatever we liked. Yet we knew from the way Jer kept moving up the ladder that he would be able to support a family. We'd been talking about having a baby since Colorado. Names had been picked out years in advance of the event. Emerson for a girl, after Jer's favorite writer. Logan for a boy, after his middle name. Whether to have children never had to be discussed. Ever since we'd hooked up permanently I'd wanted to have a baby with Jeremy, and I knew he felt the same way. Only when remained to be decided.

Though we were still living in our pug-size apartment, we started trying for a baby in 1999. All signs were positive at first. The first came while vacationing with Shari and Jimmy and other friends in the Canadian Rockies. It was after a day of heli-skiing, which, speaking of squandering money, is an excellent way to squander. A helicopter takes you to the summit of the mountain, where you jump off. There's no way up there but by air, which means you're guaranteed untouched deep powder, snow like frozen sugar that you float through. Heli-skiing was worth every penny, a real high.

That night, I did one of those pregnancy tests. Shari knocked, and when she came into the room she found us smirking like criminals.

"What are you guys *up* to in here? You're doing something sick, aren't you?"

"Look at thi-is." I held up the little blue stick. There was a round of screams. Early days for the baby, but who could tell?

Seven weeks and one day later, I started bleeding, which is not all that unusual, some pregnancies involve bleeding. Still, I went for a doctor's visit, two doors down from our apartment. I had always liked this doctor because she was our age, which was exactly the reason Jeremy didn't like her. Too inexperienced, he thought. Blood was taken for routine tests. I returned for the results and a follow-up on

Monday and they took more blood and said come back Wednesday for yet another blood test. On Wednesday they did an ultrasound and saw no baby. But they said they weren't certain, it could also be an ectopic pregnancy, and therefore to make certain—and avoid the burst fallopian tube that could ensue if it were ectopic—they wanted me to go to the emergency room for a shot of methotrexate, a highly toxic chemotherapy drug that would induce an abortion.

Your father was in Boston. The doctors made it sound like this needed to be done right away. I called Jer, who said to set it up for as late as possible, but to wait for him to get back before they gave me the shot. He promised he'd be there for that. Then I called Diana Dobin at her office on Seventh Avenue and Twenty-ninth Street.

"I've got to go to the emergency room to be injected with a toxic substance. Want to come wait with me?" I said.

"What?"

I explained that I had lost or was about to lose the baby and I couldn't face the hospital alone.

"Of course I'll come," she said.

Diana walked right out of work, which was wonderful— then again, the company belongs to her family, so it wasn't a huge issue. We sat in the emergency room at Lenox Hill, on the east side of Manhattan. I told her how Jer had been all over me on the phone. "Tell Diana not to leave you till I get there." He said it about five times.

"Right, like I'd ever leave you," she said. "Like I'm going to walk out on you in the emergency room."

I laughed at that. Diana and I talked and the doctors did

a few pokes and pricks and then Jer strode through the doorway, having taken a cab direct from airport to emergency room. He held me while I got sick to my stomach after the shot. And we held each other in the cab home. Perhaps some of our shock was not only at losing the baby—after all, it had been the very beginning of the pregnancy—but at the somewhat grisly procedure I'd been subjected to. Still, we knew it was early in the game, and within a few days we were able to convince ourselves that this could have happened to anyone.

"No jumping out of helicopters next time," Jer said.

I decided to try a new doctor, Dr. K., also a woman, who, after reviewing the records, didn't think it had been an ectopic pregnancy—which meant I'd been subjected to that ghastly shot for no good reason. She told us to wait three months and try again. We were excited at that, and could hardly wait the three months. Again, I got pregnant. And seven weeks and one day later, I started bleeding. I had another ultrasound. There was no baby.

Dr. K. reassured us.

"You don't have any risk factors. You don't smoke or drink. You're in great shape. You're a perfectly healthy twenty-nine-year-old woman. You're just having some bad luck."

Once again, she advised us to wait a few months, then try again. In the meantime, she wanted me to have a few tests.

We decided to take our time and have the tests and try not to worry about what appeared to be a somewhat disturbing pattern. Besides, we were trying to find a house and move out of New York, and we thought we'd resume baby-making after that was sorted out. During the summer of 1999, Jer happened to stop off in the northwestern tip of New Jersey en route to a business meeting and saw an ad in a real estate magazine for lakefront property. The lake was Greenwood Lake in the Ramapo Mountains, and when we saw the house, set into a hill just a few hundred yards from the New York border, we knew we'd found a place where we could spend the rest of our lives. We'd always wanted to live on a lake. The house was airy and open, with a brown log exterior, a fireplace, and an open porch. The real estate agent dropped us off and we sat out on the patio for two hours talking about how much we loved it and trying to scheme a way to get the money to buy it.

Jeremy handled the negotiations, which dragged on for months, while my main contribution was worrying that something would go wrong. We finally bought the house in the late fall. I quit my job and we started spending long weekends there painting and tearing up the carpeting, blasting music. We slept on a mattress on the floor, but it was our house and we were walking on air. We moved in just before Christmas, and right after we moved, I found out I was pregnant for the third time.

Everything seemed complete. I'd already had the additional tests Dr. K. had recommended, some of which were not pleasant. Long needles were used to take tissue for examination. More blood was analyzed. Jeremy had been at every appointment, and every test came back normal. The new pregnancy appeared to be a confirmation that everything *was* back to normal. It seemed we were finally on our way, but it was impossible for me not to mark the the passage of every day by thinking, *please let me get past seven weeks*. Then just like clockwork, at seven weeks and a day, the bleeding started, and we learned that we had once again lost the baby.

One miscarriage would have been trying. Two, a perhaps unavoidable freak of nature. Three was like living under a curse, a series of little deaths instead of a birth. Faced with such a string of disappointments, it is impossible not to ask yourself, am I broken? Can I be fixed? *Maybe this is my fault?* Our doctors were as puzzled as we were. Dr. K. wanted to do more tests along the lines of what had already been done. But I always came up normal. Normal blood. Normal hormones. Normal girl.

I'd done some digging in books and on the Internet on the subject of fertility. A friend recommended Dr. S., who had a radically different treatment that had evidently succeeded in producing a baby for our friend's wife along with a lot of other women who'd repeatedly lost babies and hadn't had any luck with the *why don't you just try again* approach practiced by the likes of Dr. K. One day, Jer and I sat down and talked turkey with Dr. K., whose final position was she didn't believe there really *was* anything wrong with me. And she didn't believe in Dr. S.'s theory, which said that immune system problems can cause repeated miscarriages. Dr. K. didn't think we should even bother with immunological tests.

"It's not something I really treat," she said.

She suggested we try again.

"There has to be a reason why this happens at the seven-week point every time," I said. "Do I have to have, like, five miscarriages to prove that?"

"I think we're done here," said Jeremy.

"You guys are going to be doctor hoppers," said Dr. K.

"We're going to be what?" I said.

"Doctor hoppers. Because you hop from doctor to doctor. You're the type of patients who'll be doctor hoppers."

I didn't know what to say to that, and simply thought, how inconvenient, to be a doctor with a practice full of doctor hoppers.

"Let's go hop some doctors," said Jer as we walked out the door.

I finally got in to see Dr. S. in the summer of 2000. A little white-haired man in his sixties came into the examining room. He had a warm smile, a ruddy complexion and a South African accent. He studied my chart.

"I know what's wrong with you," he said. "I'm going to run two tests. I know it's going to confirm my diagnosis."

Then he hugged me.

"Don't worry. You guys are going to have a baby," said Dr. S.

We were almost unnaturally happy for several days. As far as not worrying goes, we occupied ourselves getting special blood tests, which were done on both of us. The results were precisely what Dr. S. had predicted, and demonstrated two probably related problems. One was an allo-immune disorder. Jeremy's genetic material was so nearly identical to my own that my system failed to produce a blocking antibody and instead attacked his DNA. So in August, we had to go to a hospital in Philadelphia where some of Jeremy's white blood cells were taken from his blood in the morning and given to me that afternoon in the form of six injections, six immunizing little bee stings on my forearm. Immediately, big red welts appeared that remained for almost two months. The welts were proof that I had been successfully vaccinated against my husband.

The second test revealed that I have something called antiphospholipid antibodies, which cause excessive blood clotting and frequently go hand in hand with allo-immune conditions. This meant that when I got pregnant again, I'd have to be injected in the stomach twice a day with a blood thinner. Jeremy, who used to inject his diabetic brother Jared with insulin, had Jared give him a refresher course, practicing on oranges, as he had done years earlier for Jared's insulin injections. In the meantime, I'd started seeing a therapist, Helen. Helen tried to get me to find ways to keep the whole project of having a baby from taking over my life.

"I know all of this seems really bad now, but one day it's going to make sense to you. There's a reason why this is happening," she said. I remember how empty that reassurance seemed at the time.

By the fall, with the help of a lot of medical know-how, technology, stubbornness, and most of all Dr. S., we'd started to believe once again that we'd be able to have a baby. One Saturday in late October, I came back from town and Jeremy beckoned for me to come upstairs to our bedroom.

"Hey, did you finally paint it?" I said as we climbed the stairs.

I opened the door to find my friend Ana San Juan spread-eagled over my bed, like a human offering. In order to cheer me up after our medical misadventures, he'd secretly flown her in from Colorado and stashed her upstairs while I'd been driving around on some errands that Jer had trumped up. The three of us hugged and danced around.

That weekend, I got pregnant for the fourth time.

Of course, given what came before, it was no surprise that mine wasn't an easy pregnancy. Jeremy handled the blood-thinner injections until January, when he had to take a business trip to California, at which time he coached me on the procedure so I could take over. I was bedridden for a good part of the nine months. Jeremy couldn't understand why that bothered me.

"I can think of nothing better than someone telling me to lie down," he said. He fixed me up with a computer Scrabble game so I could play 200 games of Scrabble a day. If I wanted ice cream, he got it, and if I lost my mind because it was the wrong brand, he went out and got another. By now, Jer had left Giga and joined a web management firm, but this one also allowed him to work from home, so if I needed him, he was there. It would be hard to complain about my treatment as a pregnant invalid.

Early on, I went for a doctor's visit. I listed my symptoms, and Jeremy said he had the same ones: nauseous, bloated, tired.

"That's couvade. It's a syndrome. You find it in husbands who are very close to their wives," the doctor said.

That made Jeremy feel great.

"You see? I'm pregnant too," he said.

He started videotaping me. He wanted to assemble a program for you called "Mommy's Suffering Tape" that would show me lying around moaning, throwing up, and giving myself shots. "When she's a teenager and she's out of line, we'll show her this and say, 'Here's what we did to get you into this world, kid,'" he said.

Since I was high risk, we saw Dr. S. every week during the first trimester, realizing with growing excitement that we were indeed going to have a baby. We saw you as a gestational sac, a little thing the size of a grain of rice. Later, we saw you as a pale, wiggling tadpole and still later heard your heartbeat, all via ultrasound. A routine test showed an elevated chance of Down's syndrome and I worried about that for two weeks until another test ruled it out. (Jeremy didn't worry about it—or wouldn't let on.) We'd promised ourselves that we'd keep the baby's sex a mystery, but I decided the medical profession owed me some glad tidings, so I asked.

"You're going to have a girl," Dr. S. said.

I will admit that I'd actively hoped for a girl. Indeed, the night before, I'd had a dream that the baby was a boy, whereupon I took an eraser and simply deleted the male sex organs. Maybe that's the kind of thing I would have written in the journal that Jeremy bought me—that is, once I knew you *were* a girl. Jeremy bought me a nice leather-bound diary, hoping it would be a distraction during this long period of waiting. But I was afraid of writing in it for fear of jinx-ing yet another pregnancy by seeming too certain of the outcome. Then we decided we'd collaborate and try to col-lect our thoughts in a series of "letters to Emerson" to show how much your impending appearance awed us. But everything was so complicated and difficult that we never got around to it. Until maybe a week before you were born, when I pulled out the journal and said, "Honey, we have to start our letters to Emerson." But Daddy was doing some-thing else, so we missed that chance too. And now, of course, I wish so much that there had been a first letter, one co-authored by your father.

The most extraordinary thing about your birth was that it took place at all after two years of failed efforts. And it would perhaps have been too much to expect that all would go normally at the end, and it didn't. At thirty-six weeks, the doctors decided you weren't growing properly and that birth would have to be induced. We went into Mount Sinai Hospital in New York on Sunday evening, Father's Day, 2001. A very young man with a pronounced facial twitch came into the room to give me the epidural anesthetic and was severely interrogated by Jeremy. How many epidurals had he done? Starting when? How old was he anyway? Je-remy stood over him while he did it after reminding him none too subtly that this was his wife.

"Jesus, just put it in," I said.

The birth happened quite quickly, despite assurances by the doctor that no, the baby couldn't possibly be coming yet, and that since this was my first, it would take several more hours. Minutes after this speech, out you popped, tiny and way ahead of schedule as the doctor ran back into the room. Jeremy watched, wide-eyed, as a little jigsaw puzzle of a head came into view. The next thing he knew, you had turned your head around, and your eyes were locked onto his. He started to cry. And from that moment until we left the hospital, he never took his eyes off of you. He insisted on walking with you when they took you to the nursery, and being there while they cleaned you up and gave you your shots. He was fearful that somehow they would mix you up with another baby. And all the while I was muttering, "Just get me to bed. I need some drugs or something."

All that day, Jer seemed to be glowing or floating, or maybe both.

"Look at her," he said to Shari when she came up to our hospital room. "Look at what we made."

If Jer was ebullient, I was scared stiff. Like many new mothers, I was daunted by the growing realization that I knew absolutely nothing about taking care of a baby. Especially such a tiny baby, barely four pounds, a premature creature the size of a largish kitten curled up under a blanket. Various lactation experts invaded our hospital room to make sure that my milk was flowing and that we could figure out some way to feed you, all of which made me even more nervous, because since you were a month premature, you had no sucking reflex and couldn't breast-feed.

Jeremy, however, was completely in his element, and calm. He'd often helped with his little sister Joanna when she was a baby. He knew how to hold you, he knew how to diaper you, he knew how to soothe you. He knew everything and I knew nothing. He taught me how to mother you. He just took over.

Jer quickly devised a little tube that he taped to his pinky. He put it in your mouth and pumped milk into you with a small syringe. Once we got you home you needed almost constant care, including hourly feedings, so we fell into a routine where I would sleep from 9:00 P.M. until 2:00 or 3:00 A.M. while Jeremy looked after you, and then I'd take over. When I awoke, I'd find him laying on our big red couch with you sittting in the palm of one of his giant hands, sucking away on his pinky.

"Isn't this amazing?" he'd say.

You developed jaundice and we had to take you to a local hospital for a blood test. They pricked your foot to take blood and you screamed. I couldn't stand it. I ran into the bathroom and put my hands over my ears. When I came out, Jeremy was cradling you, sitting on the edge of the examining table with his finger in your mouth, and though your feet were mottled purple from the blood-drawing, you looked as though nothing had happened.

During the ride home, I asked him how he could stand it.

"Well, I love her, what am I going to do? I have to be calm for her."

Though he never criticized me for my loss of nerve, by watching him, I realized I could put aside my fear. This was when I dubbed him Daddy Milk-Fingers, though when we first brought you home from the hospital, it was as though he were Mommy and Daddy both. You slept on his chest in our bed because you didn't like your bassinet, and he got so used to having you there that one night, I woke up to find him half-awake, groggily waving a pillow in the air, shouting, "What is this? What is this?"

"It's a pillow," I said.

"Oh my god. Where's the baby? Where's the baby?" he said.

"She's right there," I said, pointing to the bassinet, where we'd placed you in an effort to get you used to it.

It took me a few minutes to calm him. He'd evidently missed the sensation of having you on his chest and had a nightmare in which he rolled over in his sleep and crushed you.

Not seeing you for even a single day bothered him. He'd come back from work excited because now he could feed you and carry you around and change you, a process that took a half hour because he talked to you the whole time, convinced you could understand him.

In July, he went on a four-day business trip to California. When he returned, he swore he'd get a job where he didn't have to fly to the West Coast because so much time was wasted in travel and he felt you'd changed while he was away.

He took a lot of time off in August to be with us. Sometimes I had to order him to go to the little office he had rented a mile and a half away so he would get his work done. We had guests every weekend, especially friends like

Diana Dobin and her little sons, Jake and Caleb, or Jer's sister Jennifer and her sons, Daniel and T. J. Jeremy would take the kids out on his new speedboat and drive as fast as they could stand it across Greenwood Lake. Having a house on a lake with a boat was a fantasy come true for Jeremy, who liked the idea of being the fun uncle all the kids wanted to visit. And he wanted you to be the kid other kids wanted to visit. Because he was in many ways a big kid himself, who would go out and buy the biggest boat and the biggest TV and wanted everything faster and louder. This culminated in him getting a huge black pickup truck, one of those things that's three times wider than it needs to be.

"You're the upscale redneck," I told him when he drove it home.

"This truck is *me*," he retorted.

It was my more comfortable Jeep, however, that we took to see my ailing grandmother, my mother's mother, in Newport, Rhode Island, on August 29th. I was close to my grandmother, and she'd known Jeremy in high school, and thought of him as a grandson. Jer took time off from work, though it was a busy time for him. As sick as she was, my grandmother was nevertheless completely aware and smiled at you and talked with us. Afterward, we had a big, fat lobster dinner and walked around a little. Jer thought Newport was beautiful and that we should come back sometime in the fall. We drove home that evening and, late that night, my grandmother died quietly in her sleep. She'd been so worried about my pregnancies that it was as though she'd only been waiting to see you before she passed away.

The next weekend was Labor Day. Our anniversary was

at the end of August and Jeremy's birthday was September 3rd. We decided to have one multipurpose party to celebrate them all at once, knowing that the day after the party we'd have to jump in the car and return to Newport for my grandmother's funeral. We decided to make it a huge party, with fifty friends and relatives. It was quite a spectacle. Jeremy appeared briefly in a Green Lantern costume. There was wake boarding off of the boat, and a barbecue that almost turned into a very expensive grease fire, with huge steaks being rescued from the flames and rushed to safety. You appeared, in a white cotton dress with ducks on it. It was like parties from years past, except now there were baby monitors.

We hardly slept that night, getting up well before dawn for the memorial mass. And we stayed overnight in Newport after the funeral. As we drove home through Connecticut on Interstate 95, I said, "You know, we've never really talked about death. Have you ever thought about what you'd want when you die?"

"Well, I don't want a big, sad memorial service. I want it to be pretty quiet," Jeremy said.

He thought a while.

"I don't want to be buried in the ground," he said finally.

"What do you want me to build you, a big mausoleum?" I laughed.

"No," he said. "I can't explain it. I just don't want that."

It was a strange conversation. It wasn't like he had some particular desire to be cremated. He couldn't seem to figure out what he was trying to say. I don't know precisely what I had anticipated, perhaps a simple factual outlining of funeral options, but somehow this conversation did not go as I'd expected. We changed the subject without ever talking about my preference.

That week, we spent our time together out of doors. I'd be tired when Jeremy returned from work but he'd say, "Get up. We're going for a walk." And every evening, we'd go to the Ringwood Botanical Gardens, a few miles away, or hike a little ways up a trail in the Ramapos. Jer talked about taking you camping the following summer. "She'll be big enough," he said. "We'll take her to Surprise Lake," which was actually a mountain overlooking a lake with a trail leading to it that we particularly enjoyed hiking. From the summit, Jeremy would point into the haze in the distance, where you could see a boxy jumble that might be the Manhattan skyline, and say, "That's the World Trade Center." I believed him, but it was always so indistinct that I don't think any of our friends did.

That Saturday, September 8th, I had to go into Manhattan for some training at my business college, where my duties would now consist exclusively of teaching the social sciences over the Internet, a perfect job for a full-time mother. I was a little excited because I was leaving you for the first time to go back and do something I'd done before I had you, something exclusively mine. Jer would stay home with you. I was wearing a sundress, and just before I left he looked at me and said, "You're so *hot*." And I grinned and realized I was finally fitting back into my pre-pregnancy clothes so it wasn't an empty compliment.

I drove into Manhattan and called him on the cell phone from a red light in Times Square.

"Emmy's playing in the crib. Listen," he said. You were giggling.

Suddenly, for no apparent reason, I felt frightened, like something wasn't right. I thought, *My God, a bomb could go off right now. Right here in Times Square.* I didn't want to be where I was, in the middle of the city. I wasn't comfortable, which was strange, because being in Manhattan had never made me feel ill at ease before. I finished my training session as fast as I could and drove home.

Oma and Opa were there with you and Jeremy, and everyone was feeling quite sunny when I got home. After Oma and Opa left, we watched a movie and I realized that you were eleven weeks old now, and things were finally be-coming a bit less difficult. I was doing better physically. You were starting to sleep through the night. Jeremy, who felt ill-used at his Internet services company, had been out on some interviews that had gone well. One job would have paid an enormous salary, in the mid-six figures, but would have meant constant travel. At the other company, he could continue to structure his own time. After the movie, he told me he was sure both companies would make offers.

"You know, if it's okay with you, I'm going to take the one that's less money because I want to be here with you and Emerson. I mean, we do okay with the money that I make now," he said.

I agreed. We did more than okay. We had everything we needed and not a few luxuries. I was proud of him. He'd come to the right decision completely on his own.

Although Sunday, September 9th was rainy and cloudy,

the good mood continued. I could feel everything coming together for us, and we just lay around the house with you and didn't answer the phone. I bounced into the living room at midday with my digital camera and found Jer stretched out on the couch with you on his chest, Maxine, our original pug, on his leg, and Eloise, our newer pug, at his feet.

"Take pictures, take pictures," he said.

"Jer, do you know how many pictures I have of you lying in this position with the baby and two dogs on you?" But I took some anyway. And we talked about how we'd go back to Newport in a few weeks, and how I'd get to go skiing this year, which I couldn't the previous winter because I was pregnant. We talked and laughed and watched you and went to bed early.

The next day, September 10th, was a busy day for Jeremy. He had a job interview in Newark, and then he was going to catch a flight to California for a business trip, one he was taking very reluctantly. We'd had a long conversation about it the previous week, and he was convinced his company, which was laying people off, would soon do the same to him, so why should he bother making the trip? But I doubted they'd fire him, he was doing too well for them. I told him he had better go. I would take you up to Windham and he could meet us there when he got back.

He particularly wanted to take care of you that morning, so he fed you your milk, then bathed and dressed you. For some reason I can no longer remember, we switched vehicles. He would take my Jeep to Newark. He packed up both cars, transferred your car seat from the Jeep to his pickup, tucked you into it and kissed you. Then he stood in the street in front of the house waving as we drove off.

The drive to Windham was uncomfortable. It was hot. You cried a lot, and I had to go to the bathroom but felt I couldn't stop because how could I drag a baby and two pugs into the restrooms? I didn't see how I could leave anyone in the truck in that heat. *This is insane,* I thought. *How do single mothers do it?* When I got to Windham, Jeremy called, excited because his interview had gone smoothly. Forty-five minutes later he called again, pissed off because his flight from Newark airport to San Francisco had been canceled due to a fire at Newark.

He didn't want to take the next available flight and get into California at two in the morning.

"Screw it," he said. "I'm going to go home, get a good night's sleep, and I'll just get up early tomorrow."

I was bummed out because now he was at home and I was in Windham and I just wanted to be with him. We talked three or four more times that night. You were crying and carrying on and I told him I wished he was there because he could always calm you. It didn't look like I'd get a lot of sleep. He planned to turn in early to be up in time to grab the first flight to San Francisco from Newark. United Airlines Flight 93.

The first thing I remember when I woke up Tuesday morning was trying to figure out whether to go out and buy coffee. There wasn't any and I was annoyed that I might have to go out and get something that I took for granted would be there in the morning. And which I really wanted because, just as I'd suspected, I'd been up with you much of the night and was tired.

I was in the kitchen, thinking about coffee and fumbling with the lid of the donut box when I heard my father say something about the World Trade Center from the living room, where the TV was. And I looked in and saw the image of the fire poking through the blackened holes in the tower's silver skin. You saw people waving shirts from the windows and felt the terrible sensation of height. Then you saw people on the ground watching. A blond guy in a blue suit next to a paramedic next to a guy in a white muscle shirt, all staring up.

The phone rang, and my dad said, "Oh, thank god it's you." I ran into the living room. He held out the phone.

"Jeremy," he said.

I looked at him.

"Oh my god, that wasn't Jeremy's plane, was it?" I said it twice, even though it made absolutely no sense that he could be on the phone if his plane had just driven itself like a harpoon into a skyscraper. I guess I said it because my dad was so pale.

I grabbed the phone.

"Jer."

"Hi. Listen, there are some bad men on the plane."

"What do you mean?"

"These three Iranian guys took over the plane. They put on these red headbands. They said they had a bomb," he said. "I mean, they looked Iranian."

I was crying, not completely irrational but on the cusp.

"I love you," he said.

"I love *you*," I said. This is the part of the conversation I don't know how to tell you about. The best I can do is this: Think of someone you love very much. Think of me. Think of the way you think of me, someone you love very much. Imagine saying good-bye to that person for the last time. Now say 'I love you' to them.

That's what it felt like.

After we'd said I love you for four or five minutes, I was in a different place. It was like we had meditated together. Physically, I was shaking and nauseous, but at the same time I knew I could make myself do what was necessary to help Jeremy play this very strong game of chess against unknown but dangerous parties.

Jer stopped saying I love you.

"I don't think I'm going to make it out of here.

"I don't want to die," he said.

"Fuck," he said.

I'm not really sure if he said *fuck*. "Fuck" is where he was though, his state of mind.

I told him he was being silly. "You're not going to die," I said.

"Jer," I said.

"Yeah."

"Put a picture of me and Emmy in your head and only have really good thoughts."

"Yeah," he said.

"Don't think about anything bad," I said.

"You've got to promise me you're going to be happy," he said. "For Emmy to know how much I love her. And because whatever decisions you make in your life, no matter what, I'll support you."

I have to admit that this just bounced right past me without leaving a dent. It was outside my frame of reference to believe anything as terrible as a hijacking could happen to us, much less one that ended catastrophically. Because everything had been going *so well*. We were together, we had a baby, we had our house. But he was planning for two possible outcomes, not just the happier one.

I said nothing.

At this point, apparently, Deena Burnett told her husband Tom, who was sitting near Jeremy, about the World Trade Center. Both towers had been struck, but neither had collapsed.

"One of the other passengers said they're crashing planes into the World Trade Center. Is that true?"

I was standing by the couch watching it on the giant screen TV. Do I tell him?

"Are they going to blow the plane up or are they going to crash it into something?" he almost screamed at me.

"They're not going to the World Trade Center," I said.

"Why?"

"Because the whole thing's on fire."

"You think they're going to blow up the plane?"

"No, I don't think so." It actually felt good to say that. Like, finally, something we can be certain about.

My dad had by now retrieved a cell phone from his car and Mom had gotten a 911 guy on the line. Hands were being waved at me that I should relay information from Jer to the 911 guy and vice versa, and I came into the kitchen with the portable phone, which has an antenna and a base unit. I conveyed questions from the 911 guy to Jer and directed his responses back the other way, via Mom.

"Where are you?"

"We've turned, we're not going to California anymore. I'm pretty sure a minute ago we went by Pittsburgh, and I think now we're going south."

"What do you see?"

"I can see a river. We're flying high, I think, yeah, we're high up, but you can see it's definitely rural down there."

He said there were maybe thirty or thirty-five passengers. He said he was calling me on the seat-back phone, not his cell. He'd left everything up front when all the passengers were herded to the back of the plane immediately after the hijacking. For some reason, however, no one was guarding them back there, so your daddy was able to speak in a normal tone of voice, without whispering.

Passing information back and forth like this just wasn't working for me at all. I wanted to help, but this way of doing it wasn't time efficient, and it was a major distraction from what I felt driven to do, which was just talk to Jeremy. After a while, I couldn't deal with it any more and I ignored the 911 guy and asked my own questions.

"What about the pilots? Has there been any communication?"

"No. These guys just stood up and yelled and ran into the cockpit. We didn't hear from the pilots after that."

He didn't tell me they'd stabbed a passenger and probably a stewardess. He could have been protecting me even though he knew the pilots were dead. Maybe he didn't know all the things that had happened. Jer tuned out on planes. He always flew with a pair of oversize headphones. He put them on as soon as he took off and listened to music. He wouldn't have been one of those people who's looking all around the cabin. I could imagine Jer sitting there half-asleep, kind of being startled awake.

"Who's flying the plane?" I asked.

"I don't know," he said.

Just then, we saw something about a plane crashing into the Pentagon, and I thought, thank god it's not Jeremy's plane.

I told your daddy about this new attack.

"Fuck," he said.

The Pentagon was probably the jolt that made Jer see quite clearly that his fate and that of his fellow passengers in the rear of the plane were completely in their own hands. The alternative was to sit and wait for the flying bomb they were riding to be detonated.

"Okay, I'm going to take a vote," Jer said. "There's three other guys as big as me and we're thinking of attacking the guy with the bomb. What do you think?"

"Do they have machine guns?" My mind summoned up a stereotyped Iranian hijacker with an AK-47.

"No, I didn't see guns. I saw knives. I don't know how these people got on the plane with what they have," he said.

I didn't really know what to say to that.

"I still have my butter knife from breakfast," he said.

We laughed.

"I know I could take the guy with the bomb. Do you think it really is a bomb?"

"I don't think so. I think they're bluffing you."

The whole time, I never heard anything come out of the other end of the phone except your daddy's voice, which was clear as a bell, like he was in the next room. I had no sense of what was happening in the background. There must have been a moment when he polled "the three other guys as big as me," but if he told me about it, it didn't stick in my memory. One of the twin towers collapsed some-where during this interval, but I don't recall mentioning it or even knowing about it.

"Okay, I'm going to do it," he said.

I knew that was the only decision that made sense. There was no question in my mind that Jeremy could take down some guy with a knife.

"I think you need to do it. You're strong, you're brave, I love you," I said.

"Okay, I'm going to put the phone down, I'm going to leave it here, and I'm going to come right back to it," Jer said.

I handed the receiver to my dad, ran into the bathroom, and gagged over the sink.

When Grandpa put the phone to his ear, there was nothing for two or three minutes. Then he heard screams way off in the background. And he thought, *They're doing it. It was bound to be noisy.* Perhaps a minute and a half after that, there was another set of screams, quite muffled, that he thought sounded like people on a roller coaster. Then silence.

Ten minutes later, an operator broke in to say that the FBI wanted him to stay on the line because it was the only remaining connection to the plane. Grandpa took the phone outside, by the stone wall at the boundary of our yard. He stood there for two hours. Then he brought the phone back in and hung up.

I opened the bathroom door and found myself surrounded by emergency medical technicians who checked my pulse and advised me to lie down. Evidently our 911 call had summoned them. I told them to get the hell away from me. I snatched up my purse and car keys and told my mom to keep an eye on you because I was going to meet Jeremy's plane.

"Where do *you* think I should drive, Mom? You think he'll come in at Newark? Or do you think they'd bring them into Philadelphia?"

"Lyzzy, you need to stay here," she said.

I didn't push it. I thought, *Mom's right. I'm breast-feeding every few hours. I really can't leave.*

I sat on the living room couch. Someone had turned off the TV. I ran through the various possible scenarios. If the plane did crash, maybe he has no legs. That's fine. Or if he's burned over 90 percent of his body, that's all right, I'll take care of him for the rest of my life. I don't care. I used one of the emergency workers' phones to call Oma and tell her what I knew. I managed to reach Jimmy and Shari, my dear friend from my trip to Australia, and Kim and Diana Dobin, and people began to make their way up to Windham.

A minister appeared from the local Presbyterian church, a woman.

"I heard there were survivors," she said.

I thought, well, of the thirty-odd people on the plane, of course Jeremy will be among the living. That fit nicely with the rest of my thinking. The minister brewed some tea and prayed, a rather formal kind of a prayer. All my energy seemed to have deserted me. I sat on the couch like a catatonic and drank tea. After a while, I got up and headed for the kitchen and almost collided with Grandpa coming the other way. He must have just hung up the phone. He was crying. He gave me a hug.

I watched him cry, a bit dumbfounded.

"Wait—you think he's dead?"

He couldn't manage anything but to cry harder. I must have asked the same question five times. I was trying to figure out how we got to this place from where we were before. What exactly had happened? When it sunk in, as it should have hours earlier, I collapsed on the floor.

I remember very little after that. Our friends straggled in throughout the afternoon and evening and they all stayed at the house. Shari slept in the bed with me. We lay there with the lights out, holding each other. It was pitch black, but there were these little sparkles above us, an irridescent dust, like a presence.

"Do you see what I see?" Shari said.

"It's like golden dust," I said.

"Yeah."

"It's him," I said.

"Yeah, I know," Shari said.

I turned on my side and it felt like he was spooning me, cradling my body in his from behind.

Your Father's Voice

Take pictures! Take pictures! Jer with Eloise and
Emmy at Greenwood Lake house. Last photo of him
taken by Lyz, September 9, 2001.

Dear Emmy,

I slept deeply, in a kind of blackout. When my eyes opened again, it was with the immediate realization that I would never see Jeremy again. He hadn't kept his promise. He never came back to the phone.

That was the morning of September 12th, the morning I stood over your crib, when I woke up in a place I'd never been before, where you're alone and you'll never be anything other than alone and you know it. Seeing you broke the spell, and believe me, it *was* witchcraft and it was pulling me under. It seemed Helen my therapist was right. There was a reason we had to struggle so hard to have you. Had it been easier, had the pregnancy not been so complicated and your early life so fragile, I might not have known how to value you.

But I didn't get all those insights that morning. I came downstairs and found an awful lot of people in the house, friends and family and a few faces I couldn't even identify. I wanted to sit and think and—strange though it may sound after what I've just told you—be by myself. Grandma managed

to finagle the key to the old stone church where Jeremy and
I were married, about seven miles from our house. As I
bounced along in Jer's black pickup, I wondered what the hell
I was doing and why I would ever think that going there
would make me feel better, and I thought how rarely I'd been
by myself since I got married. But when I saw the brown
granite of the church and unlocked its gnarled front door I
was glad. A little light trickled in from a stained-glass window.
It was cold and damp. The church is small, one room, and
filled with brown chairs instead of pews. It's not a church you
kneel in, it's a church you sit in. So I sat.

That's where I had my first conversation with your
daddy. I cried a lot. Yet it was an optimistic talk. Everything poured out of me. Thanks, I said, for everything, meaning everything good in my life. For putting me first. For
calling me that morning even though it must have been
agony to do it. I asked for his help, told him I didn't know
how the hell I was going to make it without him. And off I
went, doing what I've been doing ever since. Making your
daddy my personal saint, my private deity, the little piece of
god that I talk to.

I reminisced with Jeremy. About our wedding, chuckling
at how sweaty his hands were when we stood before Reverend Yon in that very church, how the sweat dripped on
the floor but he tried to blame it on me, saying it was *my
hands* that were dripping. Silly things like that. And so you
see, I went right back in time to our wedding, and really felt
like I'd done a little time traveling, just by joking with him
about it. Being alone in the tranquil semi-dark made me
feel as though my communication was protected, that noth-

ing could block it. I felt lucky for that peace, which increased my share of it.

I was in the old stone church for two hours, praying and crying and talking and sometimes just breathing.

When I got back to the house, I found I was in a better frame of mind than some of the people I'd left behind. Jimmy Best was sitting around, saying little, looking like hell. Kim Bangash too.

"I can't be here. I can't look at you. I can't look at Emmy," Kim said.

I told him he had to stay.

"What would Jeremy expect of you?" I said. "We're going to get through this and it's not going to be about pushing him away."

Grandpa told me he'd started crying while driving a load of garbage to the dump and the dump people didn't charge him for his garbage.

"I'll have to try that more often," he told me, and started crying again. He seemed to be in worse shape than I was.

That night, all the friends had a bonfire on our front yard, just down the hill from the house. No one knew what to do, so they did the things they'd always done together. They ate pizza and drank shots of tequila and gazed at the fire. I stayed away except for an obligatory ten-minute appearance. A memorial was arranged for Sunday in Windham, which required a lot of planning. Most of the logistics for these things were handled by others.

We also had the FBI interviewing us, and grief counselors who appeared from somewhere, probably the airline, and installed themselves in the house. They were my age.

"You might begin to feel angry or deny your feelings," they said.

"I feel like I'm going to explode and there's nothing you can say to me to make me feel better. And the last thing I want to do is talk to you."

Then I got up and left. Those poor grief counselors. They made themselves available to us all but I was the only one who talked to them and all I did was tell them they were useless. They must have known that anyway.

On Thursday, two days after September 11th, we sat in a huge room at Ski Windham, the lodge at the ski mountain, and were interviewed by *Dateline,* an event arranged by the Glicks. There were so many of us that we sat on a riser: Grandpa and Grandma, all the Glicks except Jonah, who was connected by phone from Japan, where he lives with his wife, and many of our friends. We were there for several hours, talking about the details of what had happened that morning and trying to figure it out. It was all about who talked to whom last and what was said and how everyone found out that terrible things were happening.

I carried around that sort of thinking for a long time: What happened? Who were these people who killed my husband? As I write this, sometime later, I find my viewpoint has changed. Not that I don't want to know what happened. However, just as I couldn't sit in a hotel room and explain to the FBI what it meant to lose Jeremy, I'm sure I'll never really make sense of September 11th. Did someone declare war on us for a principle? Because they were jealous? To show how tough they were? Did we in this country somehow overstep, push too hard, tread on ancient sensibilities? It doesn't make any difference to me. The world Jeremy and I knew was never more than a few rooms we lived in, a few places we walked, and a few friends and family we loved. Now it's gone, and no reason of state could ever make sense of why.

As far as what I learned about Jeremy in my first year without him—that proved a rewarding, if strange, experience, taking in everything from FBI agents to psychics, friends, old college pals, cities I visited, secrets your daddy told me in dreams.

I'm still finding things out.

In July 2002, I received in the mail a white loose-leaf binder from the Douglass Personal Effects Administrators of El Segundo, California, the mortuary that handled the crash. The binder was entitled "Unassociated Personal Effects of Flight 93."

It was early afternoon, and I waited until you went down for your nap to open it. Inside were color photographs of everything found in Shanksville not clearly linked to a particular person. We were to look through them and claim what belonged to our loved one. Jer's wedding ring didn't survive, but seventy other pieces of jewelry did, along with a bewildering variety of scrunchies, socks, hats, belts, bras, dresses, T-shirts, unmatched shoes, and other clothing items that somehow escaped the heat, some virtually unmarred. Then there were keys, books, gift cards, letters, photographs, compact discs, pens, medallions. Next to each item's photo was a description listing manufacturer, size, and so on. Some of the shoes were badly mutilated, disturbing evidence of the violence to which they'd been subjected. There was a length of electrical cord, a crumpled cigarette lighter, eighteen toenail clippers in various states of mangling. There were many snapshots of children, most painstakingly glued back together. These were hard to look at, but I went through them carefully. I had to stare at one for a moment before I realized it wasn't you. I was doubly thankful no children had been on the plane.

Over the next few weeks, I looked at a little more of the three-ring binder each afternoon while you slept. Since I'd packed Jer's bag the night before we drove to Windham—he hated packing—I knew exactly what he had with him. I scrutinized the khaki pants, but they were the wrong brand and size. Some 9/11 survivors claimed errant bits of clothing, like one shoe. I didn't want one shoe, particularly one I knew he'd probably been wearing, because my mind would go, *Well, what happened to the foot?*

I found a pair of his black briefs on the second page of the men's underwear. They were discolored and savagely torn, but there was no question they were his. I put down the three-ring binder, got up and walked around until I didn't feel queasy anymore, then I sat back down to finish the job. The books were near the end. There were quite a few, though many were missing sections or consisted only of a few pages. *Gray's Anatomy*. A paperback called *The Last River*. Address books. At the bottom of the page was an American Express datebook. The cover looked burned and maybe water damaged as well.

"Many travel dates," read the notes next to the picture.

"Numbers for Jim Best, Rob Crozier, Greg Fitzgerald, etc."
Jimmy! And LRC, Little Rob Crozier, which was our nickname for one of Jer's frat brothers. Greg was a neighbor.
There it was, just like the psychic promised: Bound in
leather, or what was left of leather. Jeremy's datebook.

I went back and forth through the ring-binder several
more times, but there was nothing more I could identify.
One of the black wallets could have been Jeremy's, but
every man I know has a black wallet. I couldn't see claim-
ing a sock or a key. The underwear and datebook were returned to me very quickly. I put the underwear away in my
desk in the little bag they came in without looking at them.
The datebook's front cover was chewed up and much of it
had simply crumbled away. Jer had carried an electronic or-
ganizer until dead batteries killed all his data and he
switched back to paper. Grandma and Grandpa had given
Jer an appointment book for Christmas every year since
we'd gotten back together in Colorado.

"2001 American Express Appointment Book, 20th Anniversary Edition." The pages were brown and unattached
but aside from the cover, it was intact. It had travel pictures
in it, a view of the Coliseum. "San Mateo" slanted diago-
nally across four days in July, a reference to the California
trip that made Jer decide he wanted to change jobs. I saw
names I didn't recognize, business contacts. "Online presence" was scribbled in the margin. There were a lot of
meetings with corporate clients in August. "Bristol Myers."
"Craig dial-in, Claudette, Bob"—a conference call. A picture of a Buddhist temple in Thailand near which he'd ab-
sentmindedly scrawled his own e-mail address. For some

reason, the notations disappeared in early September. The meetings petered out. The California trip he'd been scheduled to take on the tenth wasn't written in.

It was all thoroughly mundane, a record of the things he did to make a living but never told me about because he probably thought—correctly—that it would bore me. It was sad but it was also exciting somehow to see our friends' names and phone numbers in that familiar hand, the little architectural doodles, the quickly executed scrollwork and cross-hatched O's. It was better than a wedding ring because you felt him so particulary in all these little things. *I'll tell Emmy he took the ring with him and left us this instead.* Which of course is what I've been telling you since you were old enough to understand.

I put the datebook back in the manila envelope. My hands were covered with a fine brown dust. It made me think of the dust from the African mummies when I studied anthropology at the University of Colorado, just before Jeremy and I got back together for good. *Mummy dust,* I thought.

I told Jimmy Best and Little Rob Crozier and Greg Fitzgerald how their names led me to the datebook, which made them feel good. People came to the house and wanted to see it, including Grandma and Grandpa and Kim and Jimmy.

"All right," I told Jimmy. "I'm going to let you look at this. But you've got to promise you're not going to freak out or get upset. Because I've dealt with it."

He promised. Then he freaked out anyway.

"Aren't *you* freaked out?" he asked.

"I'm not looking at it that way anymore. I'm done with that."

Like I said at the beginning, you've got to keep moving. Otherwise you're dead. That has never changed.

At the 9/11 therapy group, several women had sold their houses, thinking it would help them heal. Most were happy with their decision, but one said it had been a mistake.

"I don't have a single memory in my new place," the woman said. I have no wish to judge what one of our number did, but it did make me even more glad that I'd kept our house.

A few members of our group were talking about men they had started dating, apparently just in the last several weeks. Some seemed a little nervous about it, and my first reaction was that this was a treasonous act. *I could never picture myself going out on a date. How can you be talking about this?* But as time went by and our discussions bore into the reality of being alone, and that we were women with most of life ahead of us, the prospect of remaining forever single began to seem daunting. One day in group, I came up with a new term to describe our status as widows: single married persons. Everyone rolled that around on their tongues for a while, and it seemed to fit. It sounded a lot less musty than widow, which conjures up shawls and doilies and black veils.

For the foreseeable future, however, my family unit seemed likely to comprise Ute, you, and me. When I got home from the "single married person" session, I spent the evening watching you leaping about on the mattress, screaming with laughter. Pure childish hilarity, a powerful antidepressant. You seemed such a happy little girl. Your eyes, which were blue at birth, now had turned hazel, more like your daddy's. And your skin had taken on some of his olive hue. You went to the playground every day, to music class and gym class once a week, like other little girls. Instead of a father, you had two mothers. And instead of a husband or a boyfriend, I had friends who divided up different roles. If I needed business advice, I called Kim. If it was eleven-thirty at night and I was crying in bed, I called Jimmy or Ana, because they'd say, "Okay, let me tell you about my day," and that kept my mind off what Jeremy's final moment on the plane might have been like, which had been in my head a lot.

But you were my greatest occupation, my work-in-progress, the thing that kept me from living in the past. There were certain happy accidents of similarity, aside from your growing physical resemblance to your father. After you started to talk, you'd sometimes call your head "keppie," the Yiddish word that Jeremy always used but I never did. "Mind her little keppie," he'd say. We'd joke about how fragile your keppie was and how we had to look out for it. Or there's the dark look that comes over your face when I've said or done something that completely outrages you— a look that belongs to Jeremy's repertoire. And when you find something greatly to your liking, right up your alley, you'll say, "Niiiice," just like your daddy.

Now you and I were about to go through our second year together—all the holidays and birthdays and reminders of your daddy. But you were older now, so much more of a presence. The first time around hadn't seemed real. I'd had the luxury of skipping Christmas and going to bed right after dinner. I couldn't do that this year and wouldn't want to. I would be doing these things with you. And we'd be celebrating them in an atmosphere of relative sanity. The reporters were mostly gone and the phone didn't ring 100 times a day anymore.

There was one event I hadn't gone through even once, however. I approached the first anniversary of the attacks with a mixture of foreboding and anticipatory fatigue. I got exhausted just thinking about the ceremonial occasions that a lot of people I knew were going to. For instance, the week before the big day, Jennifer and Jared Glick would be riding bikes from Ground Zero to the Pentagon. Oma called to tell me this. She planned to volunteer for the event, handing out water from a van. She didn't seem thrilled at the idea.

"I'm so tired," Oma said.

"Just say no to events!" I said. We laughed. She said Joanna, her youngest child, would join a commemoration of the attacks at her high school.

The night before the anniversary, I turned on the news and they were talking about the Pentagon, near which there was a big sign saying Let's Roll with a countdown to September 11th, 2002. I was livid: *This is not the millennium New Year's Eve. This is a somber day. Mourn introspectively. Find a piece of you that needs work and work on it.*

I had no plans to do anything official. I woke up and had a really big cry in the shower. There's a bench in town with Jeremy's name on it. I bought three sunflowers, which is our wedding flower and brought them to the bench and sat there a little while. Kim, Greg, Jimmy, and I all went out to a burger and milkshake place Jer and I used to frequent and ate his favorite junk food. When we got back, I turned on the TV, and there were the Glicks at a ceremony in Shanksville, shaking hands with the Bushes. I was so happy not to be there.

Then Jimmy and I went on a hike. We walked up a trail to Surprise Lake that Jer and I used to take all the time, the one that had recently been renamed for him, and where he had planned to take you on your first camping trip. When we reached the top of the mountain, the wind was blowing really hard. It was a brilliantly clear day, and you could easily make out the Manhattan skyline. Jer was right—you could have seen the Twin Towers. But of course, now the view had changed. I lay down on a rock and spread my arms out and felt the wind. We talked about Jeremy and we talked about the wind, and I said the wind was all the spirits who were lost that day, shouting, "We're here! We're here! We're here!" Because how could we not recognize the energy? It was like a hurricane up there. It was even too windy to eat the lunch we'd brought.

I thought about the past year, about the mystery of losing someone, how it seems that insights only come when you're not looking for them. And how the Little Man moves you around, but he never snaps the facts into the right order, so the meaning of the story jumps out. You look back and find you can only hold a few memories in your mind at a time, like chunks of ice bobbing in dark water, and it isn't at all apparent how they fit with one another—or whether they fit.

I remembered how, on our first camping trip in the Rockies, the one where it rained at the end, we had a night where it was almost as windy as it was up here at Surprise Lake. Jer was trying to light a fire in the wind, and we were sort of free-associating with each other, which we did a lot.

"I think we knew each other before," he said, breaking up bits of kindling.

"Before?" I said.

"I just mean, maybe there's a reason why we're so in synch. Such a nice match," he said.

"Maybe we saw a preview, and now we get to actually live it," I said.

"Maybe we were both broken off from the same piece of something, back at the beginning. So we naturally fit better," he said, little knowing, of course, that we actually had similar genetic codes and that this wasn't just a metaphor for how well we got on together.

When you start talking about things like this and you're out under the stars and in love—that's not a conversation to be recounted for any casual stranger. It's a type of privileged information, like a state secret shared by only two people. Jeremy loved the writer Kurt Vonnegut, Jr. Vonnegut had this idea of "the nation of two," that when two people are deeply in love, they make up so much of each other's reality, it's as though they are the sole citizens of their own country. The nation of two can be attacked, but never conquered. And it has a history, which is the history that created you, Emmy, which I've been telling you in this book. For a long time I've been trying to learn the story, especially the parts I missed when your daddy and I weren't together. And not once did the Little Man snap all the facts into place so that I could understand what it meant or even give me hope that someday I might understand. I guess I can't really tell you the whole story because I'll never know more than part of it. Over and over again, I'm looking for the same thing, some way of going back to the places we've been and the people we were, and every time I find a new piece of the puzzle, I'm full of the feeling I get when I feel him near me, like I've found a bridge leading back to him, but it leads forward, too, into the rest of my life. And even up on this little mountain where you can see the city, I'm watching and listening, because the wind is blowing hard, so hard I can hear your father's voice.

Epilogue

Emerson turns two! June 18, 2003.

Dear Emmy,

Since the first year without Jeremy, other years have gone by, and what I'd taken for granted was no more than a provisional, patched-together arrangement has come to seem more and more like my life.

Any day that is particularly associated with his memory is bumpy, but on the whole, I am mostly in the center of the road and less in the gullies and ridges—a more peaceful if less noteworthy ride.

One of the bumps came in the summer of 2003 when a "new theory" of what happened in the final moments on Flight 93 emerged, drawing huge attention in the press. On August 7th, an Associated Press reporter wrote, "Investigators now theorize that a hijacker in the cockpit aboard United Airlines Flight 93 instructed the terrorist pilot to crash the jetliner into a Pennsylvania field because of a passenger uprising in the cabin." A congressional report on the attacks, the AP claimed, "discounts the popular perception of passengers grappling with terrorists to seize the plane's controls."

Somewhere in the 9/11 Room, which is gradually returning to duty as a sunporch, I've saved you a copy of the "Report of the Joint Inquiry into the Terrorist Attacks of
September 11, 2001," which is what all the fuss was about. It
is an 858-page document of which two short paragraphs are
allotted to what happened on Flight 93. These few lines not
only fail to state a new theory, they are not and were never
intended as a coherent representation of what happened on
the airplane. The report's purpose was to account for intelli-
gence failures that contributed to the disasters of 9/11, not to
tell the story of the attacks. For this reason, the entire narra-
tive of what occurred on 9/11 takes up less than two pages.
Most of the remaining 856 describe the origins of the terrorist plot and missed opportunities for thwarting the plotters.

The AP story really rested on one sentence. "As described by the FBI Director [Robert Mueller], the cockpit
tape-recorder indicates that a hijacker, minutes before Flight
93 hit the ground, 'advised Jarrah to crash the plane and end
the passengers' attempt to retake the airplane,'" the story
states. This was a fact already documented in books and articles, but it was spun into a new FBI theory of the hijacking in newspapers and on national television, despite denials
by the FBI that this was even a different version of events
from that currently understood by the public. The truth is
that whether the terrorists or the passengers were at the
controls at the end has always been irrelevant. The FBI has
consistently said the passengers attacked the cabin, and as a
result, the plane crashed and the terrorists missed their tar-
get. FBI officials have also said they believe passengers were
in the cabin at the end, and anyone who has heard how loud

was the death struggle recorded by the black box will conclude that it took place in the cockpit itself. Beyond that, we will never know what happened.

Aside from the "new theory," thinking about the crash is a steadily dwindling part of my daily life. As December 2003 approached, and with it a deadline to apply for a monetary settlement to the government-run Victim Compensation Fund, it seemed fairly certain that like most 9/11 survivors, I would opt to utilize the fund, a course of action that seemed to offer a quicker and simpler resolution than joining a lawsuit against the airlines.

However, most of the duties that went with being a hero-widow—the White House functions, the press calls, and the rest of it—have vanished. In retrospect, I can see that those things were really only a kind of spasm against the steady pulse of watching you become a little girl. It's like the story of the prisoner whose only contact with the outside world was a tree he could see from his cell window. Watching the tree change with the seasons and the birds that nested there saved him from madness.

I remember a time when you were teething. You were in your portable crib at the foot of the bed, where you often slept during your first year. It was 2:00 A.M. You were crying violently, obviously in pain. I stood over you and rubbed your back, trying to soothe you. I was crying too. I missed Jer. I remember looking at you and realizing that you would never feel the loss I felt. And I found real comfort in that. For a while I'd been grieving for you, me, and Jeremy. As time went on, I let go of the pain I'd created for you, because I knew your struggle would be different.

It helped that the older you got, the more I saw how essentially unaffected you seemed to be by all that had happened. You were even-keeled, cheerful. You were a cooperator and rarely required discipline. There were no tantrums. I'd tell my friends, "This is God's way of saying, 'You know what? I did this terrible thing to do you. So here, have this, on the house: a really incredible personality for your daughter. Enjoy.'"

A little bit of age brought forgetfulness to you. At two, you forgot what your father looked like. Before that you'd always been able to point to his picture. It had happened several times that you walked over and touched the TV when Jer's picture flashed on it.

One day I pointed to a photo on the mantel of Jer kissing you.

"Who's that?" you said.

"That's your daddy," I said.

"His name's Jeremy," you remembered.

"That's right. He's your daddy," I said.

"Well, where is he?" you said.

I stood there like something stuffed.

Finally you said, "Oh, he's coming later." You picked up Blue Dog, your blanket toy, and walked off into your room.

It was a good thing you were always so quick to answer your own questions.

That experience served as a bit of a wake-up call that I'd have to really think about this. I was lucky in the sense that I was already getting some practice in these conversational gambits with older children. My godson, Jacob, Diana Dobin's child, is one smart cookie. One afternoon, about six months after 9/11, he started interrogating me about Jeremy. It seemed illogical to Jake that Emmy had a daddy, as I was insisting. Because how come no one ever saw him?

"She has a daddy, he's just in heaven," I said. "You remember him. He had the boat."

"Yeah, his hair was curly like mine," said Jake. "We went on the boat. We went *fast*."

He obviously remembered Jeremy fondly and he repeated the part about the boat. Then he turned to Diana and asked for a hard-boiled egg.

That was Jake, age four. Clearly such a conversation could go anywhere. As I thought more about it, there seemed no way to really prepare for it. But it was something we talked about in the therapy group. This was our therapist's specialty and she knew exactly what advice to give, which was not to tell a child too much. Satisfy only his immediate need for information, because more will only bring confusion, she said. You can get away with saying an "accident happened at work," rather than "they crashed a plane into his building."

Sometimes the immediate need for information isn't so easy to fulfill. Julian, Kim Bangash's son, cornered me in the living room and demanded, "Where's Emmy's daddy? He's dead, isn't he? What does that mean?" I had to leave the room. But eventually I got better at this sort of thing.

I got better at taking charge during your crises, too. You don't get sick much, but when you do, your temperature always seems to hit 105. This happened the night before we were to leave for a trip to California. It was the usual scene: three in the morning. You're spread out on the bed like a pancake, moaning. I'm chugging a Coke for sugar and caffeine so I'll be mentally capable of navigating this predawn meltdown. Your fever hasn't come down at all even though I've given you acetaminophen and a cool bath. All I get at your doctor's office is an answering machine saying that if it's an emergency, go to the emergency room. *How do I know if this is an emergency? You're supposed to tell* me. *What if I don't go and it gets worse?* I get all the baby books out—Spock, maybe five others. I bounce around the Internet looking for anything I can find on high fevers in children. The consensus seems to be that a seriously ill child is usually lethargic. You aren't, so we stay home and the next day finds you much better. This was the kind of situation where I keenly felt the absence of someone else who could help make a decision. But I learned how to do it myself.

Now you're my someone else. You can't advise me on health care, but you've developed a magnetic pull that keeps me from falling out of orbit.

I realized this the January after Jeremy died. This was before Ute came, when I sometimes went days without adult conversation, certainly without *seeing* an adult. I was more or less trapped in the house. For me, it was like being sealed up in the bell tower of a church with the bells going off every hour, or rather, like I was the sole occupant of a little room in my mind where I always knew exactly how long it had been since Jer died. Tuesday would come around and I would know it had been eleven Tuesdays since that Tuesday, so he'd been dead eleven weeks. I always knew when 10:03 A.M. came and I always reflected, "Well, this is the time he stopped breathing." These were obsessive thoughts that could not be controlled. I only escaped the bell tower when I enrolled us in a toddler's music class that happened to meet Tuesday mornings from 9:45 A.M. until 10:30 A.M. Every Tuesday morning, we'd be so busy whacking triangles and tambourines and singing "Coming 'Round the Mountain" with other fledgling moms and their kids that ill thoughts never had time to form.

So much for dealing with Tuesday. Since then, you might say, my life has been about figuring out the rest of the week. I needed another story to tell myself in place of the one where time came to an end in September of 2001. For such a long time I sweated and squirmed and pulled at my hair trying to come up with one. Once I was trying to kill a little time so I stopped into a beauty salon not far from the Greenwood Lake house for a manicure, a luxury in which I rarely indulge. I was not having a good day. It was the spring of 2003 and I was in the process of picking out a tombstone for Jeremy, something I'd put off repeatedly.

The manicure seemed like a way to relax, and the Korean woman who ran the shop had always seemed so nice. She didn't know who I was, and seeing the ring on my finger, she asked if I was married.

"Yes," I said, thinking that would be the end of it, or at least save me from having to explain how I became a widow.

"Oh. Your husband—what does he do?"

"He's a salesman," I said.

I kept answering each of her bite-size questions with an equally tiny evasion until almost half an hour had passed, by which time I had narrated a fully integrated alternative life, complete with favorite Canadian vacation spots and plans for new cabinetry in the den. I was exhausted and the beauty salon felt like a police interrogation room. I realized I should have told the truth. *For God's sake, put the polish on and let me out of here.*

Clearly that hadn't been the right story. I decided not to draw any lessons from the manicure, except that going to pick you up back at the house, which I now did, was more satisfying than anything I'd said or done that day. Maybe from here on out, I'll just let our life together speak for itself, I thought. I have no idea what it means or where it's going, but it's all ours.

It was nearly Easter time and we drove east across New Jersey to see Oma and Opa in Upper Saddle River. Trees were turning green as we passed through Mahwah, where I lived during elementary school. In the middle of town is a little pond where we ice-skated as children. You stared out the window at the gazebo in the middle of the little park and talked excitedly about a big plastic bunny in front of a store. I could see you in profile as you watched the storefronts go by, your dark eyes flashing from one sight to the next. We passed the Dutch Reformed Church, which always has an Easter egg hunt on the big lawn next to the cemetery.

"Should we come here next Saturday and meet the bunny?" I asked.

"Ears," you said.

"That's right, the bunny has ears," I said.

We drove past the house Jeremy grew up in, still painted chocolate brown, with the dents in the siding where Jeremy and Jonah and Jennifer sometimes crashed their bikes when they couldn't quite turn away fast enough while zooming toward the garage door. When we pulled into the driveway at Oma and Opa's, you couldn't wait to get out of your car seat to play with Opa in the big living room with the slippery wooden floor across which you can slide in your stocking feet, and you wanted to go out on the porch and see old Floyd the cat. Watching you scramble from the car, I felt myself relax for the first time all day. We went around the back and banged on the door. A swell of voices approached and lights came on and when the door swung open, you ran in without looking, and I was right behind you.

Acknowledgments

When I set out to tell my story, I did so with one intent—to create a tangible collection of stories for my daughter, Emerson, about her father. At the time, I could not have anticipated the importance of this book to me and the greatness of retelling our story in terms of its healing powers. I have so many people to thank for that.

My most special appreciation goes to Dan Zegart. Without Dan, my stories would still be locked away in my head or scribbled illegibly in various unfinished journals. Clearly, Dan is a beautiful writer, but more important, through our work together he has become a true friend. He patiently encouraged me to remember even the most minute details of my life with my husband. Dan brought my words to life and made my memories dance once more. For this I am forever grateful.

Special thanks to Bob Mecoy, who saw the power and authenticity in my story and took my unpolished concept and followed it through to completion. He believed in this book from our initial meeting and his efforts and enthusiasm never wavered.

More personal thanks are owed to my dearest friends and family who recounted their memories of Jeremy. They have helped me to once again find hope in the path ahead.

—Lyz Glick

Lyz Glick trusted me to help tell her husband's story, and to tell it intimately and truly. She never strayed from that resolve, and if our book succeeds, it is due to the bravery of that conviction. She is an extraordinary woman, a natural storyteller but a private person who nevertheless wanted to share something with the world and found a way to do it. Our collaboration was a very special kind of adventure. Over many hours of conversation, Lyz nudged me ever closer to Jeremy Glick.

Bob Mecoy, my agent, not only shepherded this book through the publishing process, but is a major reason for its existence. Few agents do what Bob does, which is to take an active hand in helping to decide what a book will be. He's a mensch who remained optimistic at the numerous moments when it seemed all was lost and who contributed in every way to the sustenance of the project.

Steven Schechter is a great lawyer, a great friend, and a great protector of writers. He always took the time to explain elements of the publishing business about which I was woefully ignorant.

Jane Rosenman acquired this project for St. Martin's Press and was always its faithful ally, making it clear she understood the book we wanted to write and would help us make it happen. When Jane left for another publisher,

Heather Jackson stepped into the breach and edited the manuscript with a sensitive hand and real insight into the emotional issues our book raised. Later still, Tim Bent and Julia Pastore patiently guided us through the final stages before publication.

My research assistant, Armin Tolentino, organized notes and compiled transcripts and was an indispensable right arm in putting the book together. He worked an immense number of hours for little money and I would never have completed the manuscript without his cheerful dedication. Just as important, Armin is a black belt in karate who has trained in judo and t'ai chi. For almost a year, he gave me instruction in martial arts to help me better understand Jeremy's mind-set. I'm grateful to him for introducing me to something I will study and enjoy for the rest of my life.

Finally, Laura Pedrick is my wife and my lady, my first reader and my last word, the reason I've been able to write two books. Lana is my daughter, born exactly two months before Emerson. I hope that someday she reads this story of a father and daughter and finds something in it from which she can profit, because without the experience of knowing and loving her, I could never have understood the great power of a father's love that is the heart of this book.

—Dan Zegart